Your Business
Your Book

Your Business Your Book

How to plan, write, and promote the book that puts you in the spotlight

Ginny Carter

First published in Great Britain by
Practical Inspiration Publishing, 2019

ISBN   978-1-78860-130-6 (print)
          978-1-78860-129-0 (epub)
          978-1-78860-128-3 (mobi)

Practical Inspiration
PUBLISHING

For Greg, Alex, and Leila – who are even better than books

Contents

Part II: Write 89

Part III: Promote 175

The first page

Why write a business book?

Writing a book is an adventure.
Winston Churchill

You have an ambition – no, let's call it a vision – and it insists on hanging around. On some days it makes you grin with excitement and on others it fills you with a heavy feeling of apprehension. One week you're raring to make it a reality and the next you feel incapable of starting, let alone finishing it.

This ambition is writing a book for your business, and it's calling you.

Let's say that one day, while this fantasy of becoming a published author is still a dream, you attend a conference. Sitting in the audience, you watch as a speaker on your area of expertise takes to the stage. As you listen to his talk it becomes apparent he knows no more than you do about your mutual knowledge, in fact less. Why was he invited to speak and not you? It doesn't seem fair. Even worse, the audience is lapping up his words as if they were spoken by a guru. As you leave the hall you pass a table piled high with copies of a professional-looking book – his book. Ah, so that's the reason he was on stage: he wrote it.

The following week you have coffee with a business friend who tells you she's expanding her coaching business to take on three new associates. What's more, she has the kind of client waiting list that most coaches would give an arm for, and to keep her workload manageable she's doubling her prices. 'That's amazing', you say enviously. 'How did that happen?' She replies that since her book came out she's been approached by people from all over the world who are interested in working with her. The marketing she did to promote it also brought her into contact with several podcast hosts and other well-known thinkers in her field, so she credits some of her success to the relationships she's built with them.

By now this book idea might be more than a dream for you; in fact, as far as you can see, it's becoming a necessity for being respected as an expert or thought-leader. And you'd be right. Think of reading this book as the first page of your new professional life. Because writing a book to showcase your expertise is a bit like creating a fresh business: one that has more authority, credibility, and viability than its predecessor. Whether you're a coach, consultant, speaker, or specialist, becoming the author of an inspiring and motivating book will give you the ability to charge more, work with who you want, and take to the stage more often. If you do any speaking at all, you know the value of standing in front of a roomful of people, but think how many more rooms your book will be in when everyone can read it at home.

There's also the satisfaction of your book having an influence over the way your readers think and behave, which means you've had a key input into their successes. It could mean the difference between someone struggling in their life or business, and them finding it easy and joyful. It could be the missing link between hope and despair. And it could light the spark that inspires someone to make a difference in the world, because brilliant books are transformational.

> *I never realised that until I read this book. Who would have thought it?*
>
> *You have to read this, you'll never think about it the same way again.*
>
> *Until I read that book I did it all wrong. Now it's so much easier.*

There's also a special kind of magic about writing a book, even before you've published it. The thinking that goes into structuring and writing it allows your work to thrive in all sorts of ways; you'll find the words you've written coming to life with your clients and customers, and flourishing in the form of enhanced results. You'll know your stuff so much better than before, which means that the next time you need to give a spontaneous talk you'll have the words already formed. Of course, you don't have to write a book to do *okay* in your work. But honestly, why wouldn't you want to be more than that?

So far so good, but there's a problem. Writing a book isn't the simplest of processes, is it? I always think a book is like a sausage roll: the end result is tempting, but you don't want to know what goes into it.

First there's the planning – the bit some people miss but that makes a world of difference. Get that right and you'll create a book that touches the most relevant people and supports your business. Skip this step and you can waste months of your life writing the wrong book. Then there's the small matter of crafting that tome so it engages, inspires, and educates your readers. Actually let's face it, there's the small matter of writing it at *all*. And finally, how do you market and promote your book so it sells like hotcakes? How do you get as many copies as possible into the hands of a willing audience, so you build a reputation as the go-to expert in your field?

It's not easy and it never was, but there's the complicated way and there's the straightforward way. This book makes it straightforward. You'll learn the secrets of writing the book your readers want, and that speaks to the question they seek an answer to. You'll also discover how to keep your readers turning the pages – no mean feat with today's short attention spans. And you'll find out what simple hooks to use in your writing and marketing so your book does the job it needs to do to boost your authority: put it in the spotlight.

I know how to do all this because I've written multiple books as a business book ghostwriter (which means I write books for my clients in their voices). I've also coached countless business owners through the process of writing and promoting their own books. These people are now the proud owners of shiny new books and equally shiny reputations. I've seen with my own eyes how exciting it is to become a published author, and my aim is to help you to achieve the same result. Because I've experienced what it takes to put 50,000 words onto the page, and I understand from my coaching clients how easy it can be to let self-doubt, sagging motivation, and sheer lack of time rob you of the dream of becoming an author. Also, I don't mind admitting that I've had to overcome these barriers myself in the course of writing this book! There are other books about how to write a business book, and many of them are excellent. But few are written by a professional book writer who also has a background in business herself.

In Part I, 'Plan', we'll take a tour through the book planning process. You'll become clear on why you're writing your book (a deceptively simple question), the tools you'll need to create it, and just as importantly, what else you require but don't yet realise – the 'unknown unknowns' that can derail your project before you start. Then we'll move onto creating your content outline so it both makes sense to your readers and covers everything you need to say (and no more).

In Part II, 'Write', we'll dive into the writing itself. This is where many authors begin, which is why they become stuck later on. You'll learn how to make writing more straightforward than you thought, as well as the crucial techniques for putting across your information clearly and persuasively. I'll take you through the editing process and give you ways to keep motivated during the hard times. I'll also give you the low-down on your publishing options, because much has changed over the last few years.

Finally Part III, 'Promote', shows you how to market and promote your book so it supports and builds your business. You'll have learned how to do some of this right at the beginning, because I'm a fan of marketing from the start. I'll also help you to avoid some of the time-wasting traps that are so easy to fall into with marketing, especially if it's not an area you feel comfortable with. I know what I'm doing here, because I worked for 21 years in marketing including three years as a freelance social media manager, tweeting and posting for multiple businesses and building their audiences online. Both the off and online marketing worlds are familiar territory to me.

By the end of this book you'll know what to write about, who to write it for, how to write it, and the best ways to tell everyone you've written it. As far as your expertise is concerned, you'll be the person who 'wrote the book on it' – the one who's asked to give the keynote, chair the panel discussion, contribute to your industry, and help more people. But there's no time to lose. If you're keen to see how a book can promote your business and give you the lasting satisfaction of becoming a published author, you need to start straightaway. Let's get going.

I
PLAN

Chapter 1

Your head space

Why you can write a book, even if you think it's beyond you

> *Risk comes from not knowing what you're doing.*
> Warren Buffet, one of the world's
> most successful investors

As the then US Secretary of State for Defense, Donald Rumsfeld, famously once said, 'There are things we know that we know. There are known unknowns. That is to say there are things that we now know we don't know. But there are also unknown unknowns. There are things we don't know we don't know.'[1]

---

[1] NATO press conference, June 2002.

Although he was lampooned for it at the time, if you read his words carefully you'll find they make sense because we don't always realise what we don't know. In your case this can take the form of a set of unrecognised, and therefore unchallenged, assumptions about what it means to write a book. If you've been putting off making a start for some time, or if you've completed your first few chapters only to grind to a halt, you can be pretty sure that one or more of these beliefs is what's stopping you.

In this chapter you'll learn how to reveal the invisible barriers to you proceeding with your book, a bit like a radiologist exposes your hidden parts in an x-ray. Then you'll be able to deal with them.

Why haven't you written a book already?

There's a gremlin who loves to sit on the shoulders of all budding authors whispering,'What'cha gonna do about me? I'm your book. I've been here a while, haven't I? In fact, it's been a couple of years. Strange how you've never done anything about me so far, apart from buy a book about writing a book (although it's a brilliant one). Maybe you're not cut out for it. Better give up now before you waste even more time.'

If that gremlin sounds familiar, you're not alone. I once asked a number of respected business experts why it was they'd not yet written a book. They gave me a whole bunch of reasons, which boil down to nine main obstacles. The good news is, none of them is real.

Warning: my thoughts on this may get you started on your book!

I don't have enough time to write a book

Which is really the same as...

My book isn't a priority

> *It would take so long, I feel like giving up before I start.*

> *I've got too much client work to carve out the time.*

Or my favourite:

> *I need three months on a desert island to write a book.*

There's no getting around it: writing a quality business book is a sizeable undertaking *because it's supposed to be.* That's why authors have a special status – they know enough about their subject to write something that has the potential to transform their readers' businesses and lives. It was never going to be an assignment they could knock out in a couple of weeks, and that's fine because it's not always the easy achievements that make the difference.

As bestselling author and business thinker Seth Godin succinctly put it: 'The book that will most change your life, is the book you write.' If you feel strongly about writing one, find a way to make time. How do you prioritise your most important work right now? Do you plan it in your calendar, incentivise yourself to finish it, or just assume it will be done and magically it happens? There's no reason why your book should receive a different treatment.

If that doesn't work, try this. How would you feel if you discovered in six months' time that your arch-competitor had just published the book that's currently sitting in your head?

I'm worried my book will have flaws

I sympathise with this. As a recovering perfectionist, I understand how easy it is to stop myself before I start because I'm worried I might produce something that contains mistakes or oversights.

> *What if there are spelling errors?*
>
> *What if I realise after it's published that I left out something important?*
>
> *What if I get something wrong?*

These are common fears, but that's all they are. As Elizabeth Gilbert phrased it in her wonderful book about creativity and writing, *Big Magic*: 'I think perfectionism is just fear in fancy shoes and a mink coat, pretending to be elegant when actually it's just terrified.'[2] Of course your book doesn't have to be perfect. What is?

---

[2] Elizabeth Gilbert, *Big Magic: Creative Living Beyond Fear*, Bloomsbury, 2016.

I don't know where to start

That old chestnut. When we're faced with substantial tasks it's normal to feel daunted. What should the book be about? Who would want to read it? How to outline it so it makes sense for our readers? We ask ourselves so many questions that we can run out of steam and give up. There are various ways to approach your book outline and none of them is rocket science; you just need some simple ground rules to get you going. I'll give you a clue as to where you'll find those guidelines: in the book you're holding right now.

I hate writing and I'm no good at it

There's no getting away from the fact that some people find writing easier and more enjoyable than others, but let's unpack this. Disliking an activity is not the same as being bad at it, and yet we think that if it doesn't 'feel right' someone on high (who?) has decreed we shouldn't be doing it. This is a story we've made up for ourselves, and it can be handy when we're looking for an excuse to throw in the towel.

Another way to look at this is as a matter of unfamiliarity. When you were at school you weren't taught how to write a book, so it's natural to feel daunted by the idea. But if you think of it as writing a short story that happens to get longer, or as a series of related blog posts, you'll realise you've accomplished something like it many times before.

On a more practical note, if you really don't think you're any good at writing it's likely this is a problem a good editor or even a ghostwriter can sort out. And don't worry too much about grammar and spelling; that's what copy editors and proof readers are for.

I don't know enough to write a book

Let's consider this for a moment. Do you help people through your work? Do you have happy clients? Have you been working in your field for a while and gained a heap of knowledge along the way? Set your stopwatch for 20 minutes and scribble down the things you know about your specialist area. And I mean all of them. It's so easy to take for granted what we do every day and I'd be amazed if you weren't able to fill a fair few pages with what you know, believe, have experienced, and learned during the course of doing your work.

No one would read it

How do you know? Have you asked *everyone?* Seriously though, this is a good time to do some research on your topic because it's true, some people do write books that few want to read. That's not necessarily because they don't have anything worth writing, it's because there wasn't a demand for what they had to say in the first place (more on how to avoid that later). Ask your past and present clients if they would value a book about your field, or survey your email list. It's worth proving to yourself that your book is in a readable niche, both for your own confidence and because it makes business sense.

There's too much competition

How many cookery books are on your kitchen shelf? If you're into a hobby, how many do you own on that? Try searching Amazon for books on photography, for example – there are thousands, many of which have decent sales to their name. In fact, if you see competition in your field it proves it's a fertile area because when people want to know about a topic they often buy more than one book on it.

I have over 50 books on my Kindle on the craft of writing, and more on my bookshelf. Yet I'm still writing a book about writing a business book because I trust I have something valuable to contribute. Plus, you have your own unique take on your subject, which means that your book can never be a copy of someone else's. Nobody has the final word on any subject.

People might not like it

I remember coaching a speaker who was writing her book with me. She'd been an academic in her previous career and was now a well-respected consultant to finance professionals (not an academic in sight). She was concerned that her erstwhile co-workers would look down on her newly non-academic writing style and privately criticise her for it; she could almost see their eyebrows arch and lips purse as they read. This was blocking her from progressing. When I reminded her that she wasn't writing for them, and that they'd be unlikely to spend their spare time reading a book that had little to do with their interests in any case, she relaxed and her book flowed once more. Ironically, after it was published she discovered it had been placed on student reading lists due to its helpful content and accessible style.

If you're feeling self-conscious as you write, turn around. Who's there? While I'm writing I can find myself accompanied by a crowd of frowning onlookers, but I try not to let them stop me. I love this comment from one of my all-time favourite business and self-help book authors, Robert Cialdini, who said that prior to writing his first mainstream book *Influence* he'd been in the habit of writing with an academic audience 'on his shoulder'. Once he realised this, he swapped it for a mental image of one of his neighbours who symbolised his new target reader.[3]

Who am I to write a book?

What all these reasons lead to is the ultimate question: 'Who am I to write a book? I'm not wise/special/famous/clever enough to do that' (delete as appropriate). Even if you don't feel like this now – and I hope you don't – there may come a point in your journey when self-doubt creeps in. Everyone has this, so don't let the outer confidence of other authors fool you.

International bestselling author Neil Gaiman had this to say about it in his keynote address to the University of the Arts class of 2012:

> The first problem of any kind of even limited success is the unshakeable conviction that you are getting away with something, and that any moment now they will discover you... In my case, I was convinced that

---

[3] Listen to the full story in 'Episode 102 – Pre-suasion with Robert Cialdini', *The Extraordinary Business Book Podcast*: www. extraordinarybusinessbooks.com/episode-102-pre-suasion-with-robert-cialdini/

> there would be a knock on the door, and a
> man with a clipboard (I don't know why he
> carried a clipboard, in my head, but he did)
> would be there, to tell me it was all over
> and they had caught up with me.[4]

If publishing phenomena like Gaiman are visited by imposter syndrome, it should be obvious this feeling of fraudsterism doesn't make sense. We have hundreds of thoughts every day, most of which come and go without us realising, and every now and then we grab onto one and believe it for all it's worth. We could think of them as taxis. They drive by in single file and most of them we let go by, but for some reason there's one we decide to hop into and listen while the driver regales us with reasons to give up our book.

'I've had hundreds of failures in the back of this cab, Guv'nor', he says, 'they all spent months writing a book and no-one read it. One woman was so mortified after she spotted a mistake in hers, she never left the house again. Another had a bad review on Amazon and it ended his career. I even had a guy in the back who went into hiding after he found someone else had written a book on the same subject. It's a bad business, I can tell you.'

It's no wonder we get derailed when we have this nonsense in our heads. I'm not a psychologist, but I do know one thing: thoughts are just thoughts, nothing more. When we

---

[4] 'Neil Gaiman: Keynote Address 2012', University of the Arts, www.uarts.edu/neil-gaiman-keynote-address-2012

realise this, we can take them less seriously. However, if this is a bit esoteric for you there's a more practical way of getting out of the taxi of doom and into the carriage of light...   .

The single best reason to write a book

I want to share with you the one concept which, when I realised it, changed everything for me. It was one of those ideas I'd already grasped intellectually, but for some reason hearing it from someone else's lips helped me to understand it. I was listening to *The Extraordinary Business Book Club* podcast, in which host Alison Jones was interviewing bestselling author and business expert Daniel Priestley. In it he said:

> In the process of writing a book, you're mining deep for your ideas in your intellectual property, so even if you never sold any books, or published the book, it would still be a worthwhile activity because in the process of writing you get very clear on your case studies, your stories, your methodologies [...] It's a process that allows you to reflect upon what you know, and formalise what you know into a

document, and then that content becomes blogs, articles, workshop materials.[5]

What he means is this: writing a book is an unparalleled way of deepening your understanding of what you do. It clarifies your thinking, encourages you to find a way of explaining it so everyone can understand it, and is a brilliant stimulator of ideas and insights. If you approach your book with a spirit of curiosity you can *enjoy writing it*. Once I got my head around the idea that creating my book would be a worthwhile task in its own right, I was hooked.

Let's take a look at what you gain from writing a business book before you even hit 'publish'. You might:

- work out what makes you special in your business space;
- clarify your ideas;
- create ordered thoughts out of chaos;
- learn how to convey your thinking clearly and persuasively in writing;
- come up with new ways of helping people;
- develop fresh frameworks and methodologies;
- evolve content for other content platforms such as your blog, online programmes, and talks;

---

[5] 'Episode 72 – Book as Business Development with Daniel Priestley', *The Extraordinary Business Book Club*, www.extraordinarybusinessbooks. com/episode-72-book-as-business-development-with-daniel-priestly/

- develop relationships with influencers who have contributed to your book;

- chase up case studies and testimonials; and

- record stories to illustrate your points, which you can use in your speaking and other areas.

Writing a book is a fascinating journey. You'll learn more about yourself and your business by doing it than through virtually any other activity, and if you can approach it with a sense of purpose and, yes, a little humility, there's no end to the satisfaction you can revel in. The value is not only in the end result but in the process. Not that having a published book isn't amazing too, of course. The feeling of achievement, the reflected glow from your family and friends, and the leads you'll generate for your business – these also make writing a book worthwhile. But they're not the whole story.

Why you *shouldn't* write a book

On the other hand, if your business is not yet well established, you might find writing a book based on it can hurt your chances of success. Here's why.

For a start, you've yet to generate the experience and case studies that will enrich it. Every book needs examples and stories to help it along; they make it memorable and personal. Recently I chatted with a woman who was launching a coaching business and she said one of the items to cross off her list in her first year was a book. When I asked why, she replied it was because she loved writing and it would give her credibility. Both excellent reasons, apart from the fact that it would be a massive distraction for her at that point. I could see it was easier for her to think about her book than to tackle all the start-up tasks that were mounting up on her desk. So I advised her to wait, which I'm glad to say she did, and I'm excited to see how it will pan out when it's finally done.

Which brings me to the other reason for delaying your book until you have more experience. Is your coaching or training solution robust? Have you road tested it on enough clients to know it's as good as it can be? We all learn over time, so it's worth giving yourself the chance to grow as a professional before you commit the time and energy to writing a book. If you're a start-up you're probably better off building your email list, generating word of mouth via social media, and networking.

This is what you could do instead: write a regular blog. That way you'll corral your thoughts and write the basis for your book at the same time. Spend a while considering your audience niche, clarifying the goals you have for your book, and keeping a note of any case studies and stories that will be perfect for it. Then, when the time is right, your book will be half prepped already.

What we've covered

- ❖ What goes on in your head is as much a part of your book's success as what comes out of your fingers.
- ❖ There are nine main reasons why people put off starting, or finishing, their books, and they're all made up in their minds.

❖ If you approach the process of writing your book with curiosity and use it to improve your business, you can overcome many of these mental barriers.

❖ There's one legitimate reason not to write a book, which is when your business is not yet well enough established.

Chapter 2

Your utensils

What you need before you start

To begin, begin.
William Wordsworth

We've covered the emotional preparation, but what else do you need to write a book? In truth, not a lot. The basic requirements are only something to write with, something to write on, and your brain. Maybe a pair of hands would be useful, but even they're not essential as you'll discover in a moment. Having said that, there are some useful things that will make your life easier when you're embarking on your book writing journey.

What you need

Unless you're penning your manuscript long hand like a Victorian novelist, you're going to need a PC or Mac to write it with. So far so good, but what kind of software will you use? Standard word processing software, such as Microsoft Word, is the obvious choice: it has the twin advantages of being both easily available and universally known, which means you can start straightaway without any fuss.

The downside is that once your manuscript starts to grow, the standard software has little way of helping you visualise it; you can't 'see' your whole book, only a series of documents or pages. If you save your work in individual chapters it's hard to gain a feel for how it's hanging together, and if you need to move chapters around or search for elements within the whole manuscript you can find yourself becoming frustrated. On the other hand, if you save it as one large document it becomes unwieldy.

The alternative is bespoke writing software. There are several options out there, but the one I use is Scrivener.[1] It's like a project management system for authors, and allows you to create separate files for each chapter but store them in a virtual binder. You can move them around, track your progress both in word count and percentage of progress, see which draft you're on, create footnotes, incorporate your research into separate sections, and export into Word

---

[1] You can buy it or download a free trial here: www.literatureandlatte.com/scrivener/overview

when you're done; I'm constantly discovering new ways it can help me. For instance, I ghosted a book for a client who decided to re-order the topics of his coaching programme after it was finished. No problem – I was able to drag and drop the chapters into the new sequence, amend some of the wording, and it was done. Scrivener is criminally cheap when you consider what it does for you, and you can trial it for free (no, I'm not an affiliate – although maybe I should be).

The downside of using writing software is the time it takes to get up and running on it. Most tools are pretty easy to use, but there's never going to be a substitute for working with what you already know, especially if you don't plan to write more than one book. So go with whatever option works best for you.

Something else you'll need is a quiet spot to work in. When I say 'quiet', what I really mean is a place where you can get on with writing in whatever way you prefer, whether it be in silence or not. For some authors a little background noise works well, such in your local cafe. I know writers who have a playlist while they type, which can be helpful if it's a relaxing, white noise kind of mix.

It's also helpful to carve out a space for you to write your book. It could be a home office, spare bedroom, or corner of the living room. Even the kitchen table is good as long as it's free for certain periods of the day. Having a sacred spot can help you get into the mood for writing because when you sit in it you think, 'This is my book writing corner, so when I'm here I write.'

The key element of 'quiet' is a lack of interruption, because once you're in the typing groove it's jarring to have a child walk in and ask if you've seen their stuffed toy. No, you haven't, but you hunt around for 20 minutes anyway. Then it turns out it's an imaginary one. There's no solving the problem of interruptions if you genuinely don't have anywhere out-of-the-way to work, but getting up early or writing in the evening can help. It's amazing how many words you can crank out when you can *just get on with it.*

How about people – do they come under 'utensils'? At the risk of sounding flippant, they do. It can be invaluable to have others who are in support of your venture, including holding the domestic or business fort temporarily if necessary. They can be someone in your family or household, but equally any person who can hold you to account and provide support. Think about your business contacts, friends, and even editors and publishers. A book coach can also fill this role, as part of their job is to keep you motivated and on track.

How long is enough?

We've covered the physical tools you'll need before you begin, but there are also some facts you should be aware of. One of the questions I'm often asked is how long a business book should be. This is an excellent point, because your book's length not only dictates how much time it will take to write, but it also has a relationship to your objectives in writing it. What's more, if you don't know roughly how many words you're aiming at you won't know how long each chapter should be, and this could result in a lack of balance.

The easy (and correct) answer is that your book should be long as it needs to be. There's no point padding out what could be a concise and punchy guide just for the sake of making it more wordy. Equally, if you have a huge amount to pack in, your book should expand to fit. The beauty of business book writing, especially since the growth of e-readers and self-publishing, is that it's a relatively new field with continually evolving rules, so there's no need for you to feel constrained by some unwritten law that says your book needs to be of a certain length. If there's a business book you admire why not count the pages, tot up the words on an average page, and see how long it is in total? That will give you a guide.

Having said that, there are a number of conventions regarding word count. It's wise to be aware of them, as your book's length will be one of the factors your readers will take into account when they decide whether to buy it.

Standard business books
These are usually 40–60,000 words in length. Business books, however, are shrinking. Time-pressed business owners would often rather choose a book they can read on a flight than spend hours slogging through it in their own time. That means a 30–40,000 word business book is becoming more acceptable, although if your book has fewer than 100 pages it becomes hard to fit the title on the spine (in which case an e-book is best). You'll also want to take into account its 'heft'. If your aim is to grow your

reputation as an authority, a book with some physical substance is a must and I wouldn't recommend anything shorter than 50–60,000 words if that's the case.

Books written for e-readers

If you're only making your book available for e-readers, it can be shorter still. On a device, books are easier to read when they're less lengthy as you can't gain a feel for the whole book in the same way you can when you're reading a printed version. My own e-book, *The Business Book Outline Builder*, is 9,400 words.[2] If this is your plan it needs to be part of your wider strategy for your book. Think about who it's for and how it's going to be bought and read, as well as the business results you aim to achieve with it.

The size of the topic

This has a significant impact on the length of your book. If you want to write about a relatively narrow subject, such as social media advertising, your book can be short and designed as a reference guide for busy people. On the other hand, if you're expounding a theme that demands more detail and expanse, such as the environmental damage caused by the food industry, your book should be longer.

Finally, I've talked in word counts here rather than pages, as the pagination is influenced by diagrams, layout, font size, and other elements (and for an e-reader it doesn't make sense to talk about page numbers in any case). However, you can assume a printed book with no illustrations, and at

---

[2] Ginny Carter, *The Business Book Outline Builder*, Marketing Twentyone, 2015.

a standard size, has 250–300 words per page; that means a 200-page book would need around 55,000 words.

Your time

The length of your book is closely related to the next question I'm often asked by authors-to-be which is, 'How long will it take to write?' In contrast with how intrepid adventurers are advised to hone their packing to the bare minimum and then halve it, the honest answer to this is: 'Longer than you think and then double it.' I've lost count of the initial conversations I've had with coaching clients in which they swear on their mothers' lives they'll write their books in the next three months. I know they really, really intend to do that and of course it's possible. But for most people, with the commitments of work, family, eating, exercising, and cat videos, this is wishful thinking.

If you must know how long it's going to take, time yourself next time you write a decent blog post and count the words in it. Then work out the amount of time it would take you to write your target book length and triple it for editing and research. You now have an approximate quantity of hours in front of you. How many of them could you dedicate to writing your book each week, factoring in the inevitable and unexpected diversions? It's best to be realistic.

By the way, your book is bound to seem like an unsurmountable task at this stage but don't let this put you off. Later on I'll be showing you ways to break it down.

Are you in the right business?

The final and essential item you need to write a business book is… a business. This sounds obvious, but I'm not talking about any kind of enterprise. I'm talking about the type that will *benefit* from a book. A book should be an accelerator for your company, building your authority and raising your credibility so you find it easier to sell your expertise.

If you're a specialist of some kind and make money from this through coaching, consultancy, or speaking, then you almost certainly have a business that would benefit from a book. If this doesn't include you, ask yourself if the topic you're planning to write about will complement and promote your expertise. I'll be giving you lots of ideas for how to do this in a while so don't worry about the 'how' yet, just decide if it's a possibility. Because if you don't stand to receive a knock-on benefit to your business sales from your book, it will be hard for you to finish it.

What we've covered

❖ Sort out the best writing software for your needs and establish a routine and place that will leave you free of interruptions.

❖ Take into account the length of your book before you start, and plan your time and chapters accordingly.

❖ Make sure you have the right kind of business to benefit from a book.

Chapter 3

Own your gold

Understand what (and who) your book is for

I'll call for pen and ink and write my mind.
William Shakespeare

You have your desk set up to perfection. You've carried out a few stretching exercises (maybe cricked your neck from side to side like they do before boxing matches). You take a deep breath and swing your arms back and forth. Then you sit down, dangle your fingers over the keyboard, and dive into Chapter 1. Somehow the thoughts seem to flow, and before you know it you're pausing for a congratulatory cup of coffee at the 1,000-word mark. It's looking good.

Actually… hold your horses.

I want you to picture two experts, each of whom is writing a book for their business. The first will finish their book without any drama, while the second will procrastinate at every milestone. Once the book's published, the first will command double the client and speaking fees of the second. And to top it off, the first will receive rave reviews for their book, while the second's will languish in low-ranking Amazon hell.

What's going on? Is it because the first author is a better writer, more skilled at their work, or has greater staying power than the second? Not necessarily. It's because the first author *thought their book through* before they began.

The average nonfiction book sells 3,000 copies in its lifetime,[1] and during its first year may only sell two or three hundred (bear in mind that these figures include five-figure bestsellers – the vast majority sell less than this). Depending on your aims, that's not much of a return for those hours at the keyboard, and from my experience of working with people at all stages of their books, much of that is down to not having the three fundamentals of book planning right. So let's take a look at what to do before you write a word of your book.

1. Decide what you want to achieve with your business book.

2. Pick your ideal readers for it.

3. Unearth the gold in your book.

---

[1] *Publishers Weekly*, 2006.

We'll look at each in turn.

1. Decide what you want to achieve with your business book

Let's continue with our tale of two authors, and this time we'll give them names. Our successful author, Sasha, knew exactly what she wanted to achieve with her book from day one. She runs a software company and has gained most of her clients through taking stands at trade shows and exhibitions. Her main challenge is attracting the right prospects to her stand, so from the start she planned to send targeted invitations to receive a free, signed copy of the book at the show. Her motivation to finish the book was high because she could see how she was going to make use of it, and she finished writing it in six months. The result was a clutch of exciting new client leads, many of whom turned into substantial sales.

In contrast Bob, our less successful author, came up with what he thought was a brilliant idea for his book. He manages a profitable and long-standing manufacturing business, and credits his success to the insightful strategies he's put in place. He also has an MBA, so he reckoned it would be a great idea to write a book for business owners drawing from his practical experience and research combined. He wasn't sure how he'd make money from the book because he didn't want to expand into business consultancy, but he predicted it would sell in large numbers and he'd therefore earn a fair bit in royalties. What did he do next? He dived into the project and wrote every day for a few weeks. It was fun, but by the time he'd made it a third of the way through he began to run out of steam, and his wife and business partner starting complaining that his keyboard saw more of him than they did. This led to him rushing the rest and publishing without much care and attention. To date, it has sold only 90 copies.

As you can see, Sasha put her book planning essentials in place at the start to establish what she wanted out of her book. Bob had only a vague goal and it wasn't realistic.

Choose which hoop to shoot at

What could your goal for your book be? It's always a personal choice, but here are the main reasons the entrepreneurs, experts, and speakers I work with give me for wanting to write one. Could one of them (or a combination) be yours?

- Help your readers
- Position yourself as an expert
- Attract more (and higher-paying) clients
- Gain more (and better) speaking opportunities
- Establish yourself in a new niche
- Build an email list
- Sell your coaching or training programme
- Gain emotional satisfaction and a sense of achievement.

The main thing is to establish what's in it for you, and here's where some people can stumble. It's normal to feel a bit weird about wanting a book for 'selfish' reasons, and sometimes I have to winkle people's business aims out of them after they've talked about helping the world and leaving a legacy. The latter are fine reasons to have a book, of course, because your book must help people if it's to achieve any of your other objectives. But they can cloak the underlying reason why you want a book in the first place, which is more likely to be one of the business-minded goals above.

Another way of looking at this is to ask yourself: 'Who do I want to *be* with my book? A bestselling author with heaps of kudos; the go-to person in my specialism; the speaker who inspires a crowd; or someone who's helpful and caring enough to share my knowledge?' Decide now what it is, and you're more likely to achieve it than if you don't have much of an idea.

Think about it. If you're not honest with yourself about why you want a book in the first place, you won't be able to:

- know who to write it for;
- decide what to write it about;
- choose a unique angle or 'take' on your topic;
- create an outline that works for your subject matter and readers;
- pick the right publishing option; and
- carry out the marketing that helps you to achieve your objectives.

I liken the importance of knowing your goals to trying on outfits. If you were to open your wardrobe right now and decide what to wear, you'd need to know the occasion. It's the same with your book. If you don't know its purpose, how can you tell if it's fit for it? I reckon Sasha would have been able to say what her clothing occasion was straightaway, but I'm not so sure about Bob.

In my experience, if you're not clear on your book's goal, this is how it tends to roll:

- your book will be all things to all people (and therefore appealing to none);
- it will have a confused message;
- it won't help the people you want to serve because it'll be too general;
- you'll be tempted to give up before it's finished when you suspect it's not going anywhere; and
- people won't read it (or not as many people as you'd like).

But wait a minute, haven't we missed something here? What about writing a book because of the royalties you'll earn – isn't that a valid aim? Sadly, no. You'll learn more about this when we dive into publishing options, but for now just take it as read that you'll be unlikely to earn a decent return on your efforts through book sales alone. The way your business book will pay dividends is through the enhanced business profile it gives you. Someone told me Gay Hendricks, author of bestseller *The Big Leap,* once said: 'I've made far more money from my book by talking about it than selling it.' In other words it's about the cachet, not the cash.

2. Pick your ideal readers

Your book isn't for everyone. This can be hard to acknowledge, but it's a good thing because it forces you to focus on how you're going to create a transformative reading experience for your audience. If your readers don't like your book they won't buy it, and if they don't buy it they won't read it. Your book will live or die on how well you engage with them, and central to that is knowing who they are in the first place. Please don't worry about excluding people from your readership – a book is always easier to appreciate when you know who it's aimed at, even if you can see it's not you.

There's a science to picking the right readers for your book, which I'll explain here. To do this I'm going to resort to fictional characters again: this time they're authors Bill Bestseller and Clare Credibility.

Bill Bestseller

Bill wants his book to be included in the traditional bestseller charts, such as *The Sunday Times* bestseller list. It's important to him that he has his name in lights: this was his number one goal when he decided what he wanted to achieve with his book. So he'll need to write a book aimed at a reasonably broad audience about a topic many people can relate to, such as how to be an effective leader in business. Alternatively, if he wants to dominate a niche category on the Amazon bestseller list, he may decide to narrow his target readership. Either way, he's taking his book goal into account when choosing who to write for.

Clare Credibility

Clare Credibility, on the other hand, is writing a business book to raise her authority in her field, so aiming her book at the specific group of people she wants to influence is essential. Given she's a consultant helping start-ups, she'd have success with a book for new entrepreneurs. If she were to target her book at *all* entrepreneurs, she'd find it harder to market and it wouldn't resonate so well with her preferred audience – this would lead to its being less successful. You can see how easy it would be for Clare to become distracted by the lure of topping the bookstore bestseller lists, forgetting that her main aim is simply to gain more clients in her existing business area. Not that there's anything wrong with being a bestseller, of course, but it would be an added bonus for her rather than the main objective.

So being picky about your readership makes the task of writing and marketing your book manageable. But how do you go about choosing which readers to target? First, work out what you want your book to do for your business. Is it to attract more of the kind of clients you already have, or to reach a new audience? If it's the former, that's relatively easy because you know them already; if it's the latter you'll need to do more research. What is it about the new audience that appeals to you? Is it because you like the idea of writing for it, or because it makes business sense? Always consider what your potential readers will give you.

By the way, you can aim your book at an audience other than your direct customer base if that makes sense for you. This book, for instance, is for experts who want to write their own book, but it's also aimed at people who might hire me to ghostwrite their book. The latter may have no intention of writing it themselves, but the simple fact that I've published a book on the subject will give me credibility with them.

Once you know who you're writing for, it's a great idea to create an avatar of your ideal reader so they become clear in your mind. In effect, Tim Ferriss did this when he wrote *The 4-Hour Work Week*; dissatisfied with how his early chapters were going, he abandoned them and re-wrote them as an email to two 29-year-old friends of his, which made it far more authentic and powerful. A vivid way of starting this process is to imagine the one person (real or imagined) who you'd love to contact you when they've read your book – this will help you to write for them in a powerful way. If you have someone specific in mind all the better, because it will help to make them real.

Here are some questions to answer which will help you create a reader avatar.

- The obvious stuff: What's their age, gender and location?
- What do they do for a living?
- How do they like to spend their free time?
- What's their motivation for buying your book?
- Where and when might they read it?
- What are their desires and dreams?
- What are their frustrations and worries?

- What have they assumed about their situation before they read your book? Where are they 'at'?

It's worth creating a one-sheet summary with a picture at the top, and pin it over your desk so it's always to hand when you're writing – that way you never lose sight of your ideal reader. My coaching clients also find it helpful to schedule a couple of chats or interviews with sample readers part way through writing their book, to make sure they're not going off track.

Streamline your book marketing

This means aligning your book's audience with that of your business. Now I know you're far from marketing your book – you've not even started writing it yet – but you'll make selling your book a whole lot easier when it's written for the same audience as your business. You should already have a promotional audience for your business – it might be people on your email list, social media followers, podcast listeners, or a combination of people on different platforms. If your book is aimed at a different audience to these, you're going to have to bypass the ones you've worked so hard to build up and start again with another. That's hard work.

Having said that, you may be writing your book with the intention of moving your business up or across a level in terms of your client base. It's important that you consider who you want to serve in the future as well as now, and the earlier you factor this into your content and marketing planning the better.

3. Unearth the gold in your book

Readers don't buy books, they buy solutions that make them feel good. In the case of a nonfiction book, your readers will have a central question they want an answer to. 'How can I lose weight without feeling hungry?' 'What can I do to achieve more in life?' 'Why is global warming happening and what does it mean for our planet?'

Your job is to provide a satisfying answer to that question, and that one only. By doing this you'll answer plenty of others too, but they must all lead to the resolution of the key uncertainty your readers started with. The unique take you have on this issue, and the special way you give your readers insights into it, is the gold in your book. *Own your gold.*

If there's ever a reason a business book fails to do well it's because its central concept doesn't grab people, but get your golden nugget right and you're set for success. If you're clear on your gold, you can work your whole book around it and also use it in your marketing messages when it's published. So how do you dig out that gold? Here are some suggestions.

Use the 'even if' rule

Suppose you're planning a book about how to create a profitable online business. Your readers don't only want to know how to sell online, they're also keen to discover how to do it *even if* they've never done it before, or *even if* they hate social media, or *even if* they don't have an online product to sell yet. The 'even if' bit is your gold: it's what makes your book irresistible to your readers. A coaching client of mine wrote a book about a niche area of IT that helped newcomers to feel like experts; his gold was that years of practice wasn't essential for professional success in this area.

Ask, what makes you special?

What do your clients say *really* helps them when they work with you? Is it your approach, your background, your personality, or something else? Because this is the difference you need to reflect in your book. Many of my ghostwriting clients like the fact that I have a business background, for instance, because it gives me an extra insight into writing books about business topics. That's why I've focused on the business benefits of writing a book in this one.

Step onto your soap box

Our strongest opinions are often our most reliable guide to what the gold in our books could be. What frustrates you about your industry right now? What trap do you see your clients regularly falling into, that could so easily be avoided if they followed your advice? What's the one thing that everyone in your target readership seems to get wrong, and you can't understand why? When you know what that is, you've struck gold. Your book stops being yet another 'how to' guide or 'this is what I think' piece, and starts to address the core issue that stirs your readers up. My key frustration, for instance, is seeing business authors skip the planning phase of writing a book and leap into the writing, then either ending up with the wrong book or giving up part way through. That's why I'm spending the first third of this book helping you to avoid that mistake.

You'll see from this that it's important to stand for or against something, which means your book won't be for everyone. To speak strongly to one group of people is inevitably going to have the result of rubbing up others the wrong way, so don't be afraid to do this. Think of Charles Darwin's *On the Origin of Species*, Karl Marx's *Das Kapital*, and Germaine Greer's *The Female Eunuch* – all works that strongly divided their readership in their day (some still do) but have come to be respected as thought-leading classics. You don't have to be controversial for the sake of it, but you do need to know your position on your subject.

Pick the killer idea for your business book

Once you have a feel for what's going to make your book special, you need a central thesis to base it on. Because your book is a branding device – it's your in-depth piece of content that explains both what you think and how you go about your work. It must reflect what makes you unique: your voice, your ideas, and your methods.

How do you pick that killer idea for your book, and how can you be sure it's the right one? I have a great set of questions to clarify this for you. Even if you're already sure your idea is sound, it's worth answering them because you might have a re-think when you do. Ask yourself:

? Does it fill me with excitement? You'll be spending a lot of time writing about your idea, so you need to love it.

? Is it supportive of my business? It needs to be an idea that will help it to grow. This could be through the extra speaking engagements you'll attract, the new clients you'll gain, or the raised profile you'll achieve.

? Is it aimed at a similar audience to my existing business, or a future version of it? If not, you'll be unlikely to answer 'yes' to the second question.

? Do I know my stuff? A successful book is written from a place of knowledge and expertise.

? Could I combine one or more of my ideas into a single book? Or how about the intersection of two? Something innovative could come out of the overlap.

? Is there a significant audience that cares about this idea? Will enough people want to read it?

If you'd like to see this process in a handy visual flowchart, you can download it for free here: https://marketingtwentyone. co.uk/idea

Understand the difference between needing and wanting

Your book must be on a topic your readers *want* to read about, not necessarily on one they *need*. There's a difference. Ask yourself when you last invested time or money in something you needed and you'll probably think of paying your utility bills or investing in a vital business software update – in other words, things you can't avoid. But once you've covered the necessities, your discretionary time and money goes on things you want, such as vacations and new clothes. It certainly isn't spent on learning something from a book that you didn't even know was useful or interesting.

This is best illustrated through an example. Carlos was a tech enthusiast who'd stumbled upon a great idea for how people with illnesses could use video conferencing to communicate with their doctors more easily. He'd researched his topic and spoken with medical specialists, all of whom supported him in his endeavour. By the time he consulted with me, he'd spent months writing a book about how to do this and was all set to publish and promote it.

The problem was that Carlos assumed patients would be as enthusiastic as doctors to learn about his subject. But being realistic, what patient buys a book so they can help their doctor to treat them? They might if the doctor recommended it, but they wouldn't seek it out for themselves – they wouldn't even know such a thing existed. Even if they did discover it, they'd be unlikely to be keen to spend their precious disposable time and income on it. They'd need it, but they wouldn't want it.

When I explained this to Carlos it took a while to sink in, but by the end of our conversation he'd come to the realisation that his book had a niche audience of selected doctors only. They were the ones who might want it because it would make their work easier, not the patients. This didn't invalidate the book but it did make a difference to how it should have been written, and also to his marketing plans. If you don't understand the difference between needing and wanting you might end up writing the wrong book too. Ouch!

Own your gold

Once you know what your book's about, you should be able to fill in the following blanks:

> I want to help [*my target readers*] to [*my expertise*] so they can [*the result for them*] and so I can [*my goal for myself*].

Here's a filled-in example:

> I want to help people who feel stressed to relax, so they can live happier lives and I can attract more attendees to my stress-reduction workshops.

Try yours now, and memorise it. You should know it so well you could mutter it if I woke you up in the middle of the night and asked you it. Do you think you could do that?

What we've covered

❖ For your business book to deliver what you want, you first need to decide your goal for it.

❖ Choosing a particular readership will help you write the right book and market it well.

❖ For your book to be irresistible to your readers, you should be clear on the burning question they have, and how you intend to answer it in your own special way.

❖ Your book must be based on something that your readers *want* to learn about.

Chapter 4

Your return on investment

Make sure there's enough in it for you

It is better to have a permanent income than to be fascinating.
Oscar Wilde

Now you know what you want to get out of your book, who it's for, and what's special about it, you're all set to think about how you're going to sell it when it's published. I'm not about to ask you to create a marketing plan just yet, but I am going to start you thinking – in a top-line way – about how you'll promote your book. Because I don't want you to be one of those authors who types 'The End' and then starts to wonder how they're going to sell the thing, only to discover that if they'd given it more thought earlier on they'd be in a far better position. You'll thank me later, I promise.

Marketing your business in your book

I'm sure you would never commit a sizeable sum of money to any venture without some idea of what you would receive in return, and it's no different with a business book. For your book though, it's more about how you're going to gain a profitable payback for your investment of *time*. As you've already seen, this ROI will most likely take the form of more lucrative clients, more fruitful opportunities, and increased connections.

This is where many business authors become stuck, because they don't know how to craft their book so it enhances the return for them. However, it's easy when you know. There are three under-used tricks to rocket your book's ROI, and they're contained within your book itself. They are:

- lead magnets;
- seeding; and
- bringing influencers into your book.

Let's look at why they're important and how you can use them.

Lead magnets

Wouldn't it be great if you knew who every reader of your book was, and could keep in touch with them after they'd finished it? You could find out what they thought about the book, ask them to review it, and impress them with your helpfulness and expertise so they want to work with you in other ways. There's even the potential to keep them hooked on your business long term.

There's a way to do just that, and it's through lead magnets. A lead magnet is a way of gathering leads for your business by offering your readers a free giveaway in exchange for their email addresses. Here's how it works: you create a piece of digital content such as a pdf or video. Then, in your book, you direct your readers to a sign-up page on your website that invites them to access the material for free when they enter their contact details. The address goes through to your email service such as Mailchimp or Aweber, which means you can stay in touch for as long as they want you to. You won't be sending them spammy or salesy emails, but useful and readable content. You could discuss some of the ideas in your book, give topical updates, and – occasionally – promote your services to them. Voilà – you have a way of keeping in touch.

You can include your lead magnets after you've written your book, but they come across more naturally if you insert them alongside the writing or – better still – plan them in from the beginning. Doing this will also give you time to set up the tech so it's one less thing to panic about at launch.

Lead magnet tips

It's worth knowing the following when you create and set up your lead magnets.

- The content is vital: it must be of genuine value to your reader, worth as much in their eyes as the price of the book itself. That doesn't mean it has to be expensive to produce – it's what's in it that matters.

- Try to gear the content towards the part of the book in which you insert the link. Lead magnets work most effectively when they're a logical and irresistible follow-on from what your readers are currently consuming.

- Ensure you follow general data protection regulation (GDPR) rules by gaining consent at the point of sign-up to the kind of emails you plan to send – for instance marketing and promotional content – and give your recipients the opportunity to opt out at any time.

- Ideas for lead magnets: templates, checklists, reports, flowcharts, explanatory videos and audios, and video demonstrations.

In terms of what web address to use for your website landing page, there are a couple of options. You can create a new page for each download, giving it a name that's easy for your readers to type (for example, www.yourdomain.com/motivational-tips). Or you can create a page on your site with all your downloads, such as www.yourdomain.com/book-materials. This is easier to set up and manage, but less bespoke. The choice is yours.

Seeding

This isn't anything to do with your garden, although it does bear fruit. Seeding is when you sprinkle some great examples of your work throughout your book, with the intention of planting your expertise in your readers' minds. Here are a couple of examples.

From a parenting expert:

When I work with challenging kids, I'm able to reduce their anger outbursts by half in the first month. That's how powerful this method can be.

From a business finance consultant:

It's never too late to start getting on top of your business finances. I once worked with a business owner who was about to go bankrupt, and by following this five-step plan he avoided losing his company.

Seeding tips

Bearing the following in mind will improve your seeding.

- Work your examples into the book in a natural way, ensuring they're in context and flow with the rest of the text.

- Don't sow too many seeds – you don't want it to look like a sales brochure.

- Be natural and confident, not cheesy.

Bringing influencers into your book

People often love to be interviewed or asked to contribute to a book; it widens their exposure to a new audience and gives them the chance to talk about what's important to them. But there's also a benefit to you, the author, because if these people are in your book they'll have an incentive to promote it to their own network.

Could your book benefit from extra content from other experts, with skills complementary to your own? Why not interview them or ask them to write a short piece to include? And could you ask permission to quote someone who you'd love to be on the radar of? I've contributed to other people's books myself and it's a win-win scenario.

Influencer tips

Here are some pointers for how to work with influencers so both parties receive maximum value.

- Pick influencers who have a similar target market to you, but who ideally aren't competitors. That way they'll be happy to mention your book to their contacts and you both gain.

- Your aim is both to enrich your book's content and attract a wider audience for it, so bear that in mind when you choose who to ask.

- In the run up to publication day, keep your contributors up to speed with your launch plans and ask them if they would consider promoting your book to their audiences. They'll gain the kudos of being in your book and you'll achieve a wider market for it.

What you can do NOW to set up your book marketing for success

Picture the day when you hold your finished book in your hands. You pour yourself a glass of bubbly, post a picture of yourself with it on social media, phone your mum, and collapse in a self-satisfied heap. But there's one thing missing at this point: a group of willing readers to buy it. Who are they? Where are they? And, just as importantly, why would they be interested in your book?

Here's where starting to build your author platform while you're writing your book is vital. The word 'platform' can be somewhat mystifying (I always envisage a diving platform – most off-putting) but think of it as a stage upon which you stand to talk about your book. In fact, you'll need multiple mini-platforms which could include, in no particular order:

- social media accounts;
- your email list;
- speaking engagements;
- your website;
- influencers who have an audience with your readers; and
- face-to-face networking events.

You can see how an author platform is simply a place from which you launch marketing messages about your book, and why it's important to have a ready-made audience who will be interested to hear about it. What's the size of your audience at the moment? Is it big enough to sell hundreds or even thousands of copies? It might not need to be huge; if you work in a niche area you don't need attention from vast numbers. But do you have a critical mass of potential readers who you can talk to as soon as your book is ready for them to buy?

By considering this in your planning phase, you haven't left it until the last minute. Building a marketing platform takes time, so start early and continue steadily while you write it. The beauty of this approach is that not only will you enlarge your audience, but you'll also find yourself thinking about your readers while you're going along – a great way of keeping that laser focus on your reader alive.

You don't have to build a base on every platform, and if you haven't done much marketing before just choose the ones you feel most confident with. As book PR expert Chantal Cooke once said to me, 'The marketing that works is the marketing you *do*', so don't set yourself the challenge of being a superstar in every area because you're unlikely to have the time or energy for that.

How to build your platform

For now you're simply building an audience that you'll promote to when your book is finished. Here are the areas to focus on at this stage.

Social media

Pick two platforms you resonate with and where you've already had some success. Don't try to do it all, but do make sure they're the places your audience hangs out. For a business book that will most likely be LinkedIn and Twitter, but you might find Facebook and Instagram are fruitful for you (and by the time this book has been around for a while there will no doubt be some hot new platform to consider). Then, build your audience by connecting with people in your target readership every day and posting messages they'll find interesting, useful, and related to your expertise. For now, this is all you have to do.

Email

What size of email list do you have? If it's only a handful of people this may be an area for you to enrich. There are many ways to increase your list: install a pop-up box on your website that offers a lead magnet in exchange for an email address, and post social media links to that page, or give a webinar or talk which allows you to collect email addresses. While you're building your list, remember to email it regularly with useful and interesting content geared to your audience. You could talk about how your book is evolving as well, and create a sub-list of people who volunteer to hear more about it.

Speaking engagements and face-to-face networking

If you speak and attend events regularly, consider enhancing your network of events organisers so when your book is launched you have a ready-made list of people to contact.

Your website

Is it fabulous to look at and use, or could it frankly do with a revamp? Now's the time to make it ship-shape so that when your book is published it's ready for you to add a 'Book' page to.

Influencers

This can be huge. While you're writing your book, build a list of people you could ask to help you promote it when the time comes, and use the writing period to deepen your relationships with them. This could involve asking them to contribute to the book, or finding ways to interact with them on social media or face to face. Don't underestimate the power of reciprocity; if you can help someone with something that's important to them, they'll remember that act of kindness. Successful coach Michael Neill tells a brilliant story about how he persuaded an ultra-busy influencer to write a foreword for one of his early books, by offering to take some of her most hated jobs off her to-do list (and it worked).

What we've covered

❖ Writing a business book should be a profitable venture, and if you incorporate certain tasks into your book and business marketing from the beginning it will be more financially successful.

❖ Creating lead magnets, seeding your expertise, and inviting influencers to contribute to your book are three key ways to gain a return on investment for your time.

❖ You should also start to build your marketing platform so it's ready for use when your book is published.

Chapter 5

Your title

Attract the right readers at first sight

A good title is the title of a successful book.
Raymond Chandler, bestselling author and screen writer

If you've told your friends and family you're writing a book (and I hope you have), I expect the first question they asked was, 'What's it about?' And the next one was probably, 'What's it called?' So it's no wonder you might feel a little fixated on your title right now. Deciding it at this stage is by no means essential, but you might find knowing it gives you a 'hook' to hang your book on and makes it seem like it's really happening. It can also be a lot of fun choosing a title, and one day it will have your name under it. How cool is that?

Ironically, I find the best way of coming up with a title is to forget about it – I just give up. Then one day it comes to me while I'm doing the washing-up, or – my favourite – while I'm out for a walk. If your mind knows it needs to generate a fantastic title, let it carry on without interference and it will eventually reward you. If you want some more concrete advice, though, here are some stimuli you might also find helpful.

- Think about the end benefit your readers will receive from your book. People buy nonfiction books because they want to solve a problem or learn about a specific topic. *Yes! 50 Scientifically Proven Ways to Be Persuasive* by Robert Cialdini makes the result clear, as does *How to Win Friends and Influence People* by Dale Carnegie.

- What kind of feeling do you want to generate? Do you want people to feel inspired, excited, relieved, angry, in control, knowledgeable – or some other emotion? If you want them to feel relieved, *Take Charge of Your Child's Sleep* by Judy Owens and Jodi Mindell is a great example because it emphasises the feeling of control the reader will gain.

- Who's in your target audience? There's no better way of letting your potential readers know they've come to the right place than if they can recognise themselves in the title. *Nice Girls Don't Get Rich* by Lois P. Frankel makes it clear the book is aimed at women who aren't confident around money but want to improve their finances.

You'll also find that sometimes the most impactful titles are those that embody a contradiction or lack of logical connection between the words – this has the effect of stimulating your readers' curiosity without them quite realising it. Here are some examples to show you what I mean:

Playing Big by Tara Mohr

The Millionaire Next Door by Thomas Stanley and William Danko

Strong Woman by Karren Brady

Wilful Blindness by Margaret Heffernan

Although there's no set formula for it, a short and memorable title that encapsulates your content and tone is what you're after. Once you've come up with some ideas, the next step is to research your competitor titles because it's important to avoid duplicating the name of a book in a similar category or field. Just enter your title into the Amazon search box and this should tell you if there's an issue. While you're online, also think about whether you have appropriate keywords contained within your title, especially if your book is a how-to guide or solves a specific problem. Imagine someone Googling 'how to create an online course', for instance. They might not even be looking for a book, but they're hungry for information. If your title aligns with the words they've entered, they may find themselves clicking on your Amazon listing and buying your book that way.

Your subtitle

You also need a subtitle. This does the heavy lifting for the main title, especially if the latter is esoteric or quirky. Even if it isn't, it's important to explain what the book is about in more detail and it's a useful way of adding some keywords. Daniel Pink's book *Drive* has the subtitle *The Surprising Truth About What Motivates Us*, which clarifies his title beautifully.

Your subtitle is also a clever way of showing what position your book is intended to occupy in the lives of your readers. Is it an all-encompassing guide to a particular area of their life, a 'starter' help book, a step-by-step set of instructions – or what? Knowing this will help you match your book with your readers' desires and expectations.

How do you know if you've chosen the right title?

Your title might come to you and feel so 'right' that nothing else will do, or you might go backwards and forwards with whether you have a knock-'em-dead solution. Either way, it's a good idea to sense check it using this list of questions.

- Does it make the content of your book clear? If not, proceed with extreme caution and pay special attention to your subtitle.

- Is it memorable?

- Could anyone pronounce it?

- Is the domain name of it available (if that's important to you)?

- Is it short enough to stand out on a thumbnail size of your book cover (on an online listing)?
- Does it contain relevant keywords?
- Is it unique?
- Do you feel proud when you say it?

If you can tick all or most of these boxes you're onto a winner. If in doubt, clarity should trump everything else; just say what it does on the tin. Remember, your title has one role and one role only: to encourage your target readers to pick it up, consider it, and then buy it.

What we've covered

- ❖ It's not essential to decide on your title before you write your book, but you might feel it helps to motivate you and keep you focused.
- ❖ There are various factors to consider when you create a title, but clarity is the key one.
- ❖ A subtitle explains the relevance of your main title.

Chapter 6

Build your skeleton

Construct your elegant book outline

It takes as much energy to wish as it does to plan.
Eleanor Roosevelt

When one of my nephews was seven years old, he proudly showed me a science test he'd done at school. My attention was drawn to a question halfway down the paper: 'Why do we have a skeleton?' His answer was as direct as only a small boy's can be: 'Because otherwise we'd be a pile of skin and organs on the floor.'

Moving on from that delightful image, this is what a book outline achieves. It takes the jumble of points you want to make and turns them into a coherent and flowing set of chapters that gracefully guide your readers to your conclusion. Without this skeleton your concepts would flop about aimlessly, veering hither and thither, confusing the heck out of everyone. This is important, because when a business book falls flat it's rarely down to the style it's written in or because there are a few spelling and grammatical errors along the way. It's because it *doesn't make sense* – your readers don't 'get' it.

Creating your book's outline can be fun. You almost certainly have some content swilling around already – it could be ideas and thoughts in your head, a collection of blog posts you've written, or the talks you've created. In the next chapter I'll cover how to choose what to say within each of your own chapters, but here we're just looking at what type of book you're writing and how its table of contents will pan out.

Outlining your book

There are two main ways to order your thoughts, and which one you choose depends on your personal preference.

Mind mapping

This will appeal most if you're a visual person. Grab a sheet of paper (or use online software tools for mind mapping) and write your book's central message (your 'gold') in the middle, with a circle around it. Then draw a line from that and at the end of it write whatever relevant topic comes to mind first, circling that too. Your next thought might be a splinter topic of that one or another main idea that comes from the centre – it doesn't matter what order they appear to you in, just keep scribbling them down and draw lines to and from the appropriate places.

Your sheet will end up looking like a demented spider's web, but somewhere in it lies the beautiful skeleton of your book. Your next task is to take a step back and work out what topic your readers would want and need to know about first, second, third, and so on. Re-draw your mind map to reflect this new, more logical order.

Sticky notes

This is my personal favourite because I prefer a linear approach. Grab a colourful pile of sticky notes and jot a different topic on each one, placing them onto a white board or sheet of flip chart paper – some will be major themes and others minor points, it doesn't matter. Don't worry about ordering them, just dump all your ideas out. Once all your notes are on there, see what themes emerge. Then draw columns on your board or paper with a working chapter heading for each and transfer the notes onto them by theme – you've made some chapters. Now you can take a fresh look to decide what order the chapters should be in, based on how helpful that order would be for your readers.

What these two processes have in common is how instinctive they are. So often I find people feel daunted by the thought of organising their material, but when they have an easy system to follow they realise they know how to do it already. The outline just needs some help with being born.

Your book type

Now you know what you want to say and in what order, you need to create a table of contents. To do this it's helpful to know there are four main types of business book, each with its own top-level outline.

1. Self-help or how-to guide, such as *Will it Fly?* by Pat Flynn.

2. Transformational memoir (your story and how your readers can learn from it), such as *Option B* by Sheryl Sandberg and Adam Grant.

3. Thought-leading, inspirational book, such as *A Good Time to be a Girl* by Helena Morrissey.

4. Collection of interviews, such as the final section of *Public Speaking for Authors, Creatives, and other Introverts* by Joanna Penn.

What type of book do you want to write? Let's look at each to help you decide; even if you've already picked a format you may find yourself changing your mind once you've been through them.

Self-help or how-to guide

This is a stalwart of nonfiction books, and is an excellent vehicle for showcasing your expertise and experience. If you're a coach or consultant, it both gives you the opportunity to prove what you know and offers your readers a low-risk way to become familiar with your ideas. As such, it's also a great option if you have a programme or service you'd like to turn into a book, as you'll gain a whole new audience for it.

This type of guide is a step-by-step process for helping your readers travel from a place of uncertainty to one of knowing, using your expertise and experience to get them there. They may be feeling vulnerable and confused, or even just looking for an improvement to their current situation. Either way, they'll appreciate you taking them by the hand and leading them gently through the process of change in a logical and straightforward way. If you want to use your book to raise sales of your programme, it's a good idea to order your content in the same way so there's a seamless join between the two.

- *Introduction*: describe your readers' problem, including how it's manifested in their lives, and empathise with them. Maybe you had the same issue yourself in the past. Explain briefly how you're going to help them solve it in this book, and convince them that you're someone to trust by showcasing your credentials.

- *Chapter 1*: lay the groundwork. This consists of the underlying principles your readers should understand before they take their first improving step (you might need more than one chapter for this).

- *Chapter 2+*: take your readers through a step-by-step process for overcoming their problem, with each major step having its own chapter. Include action points, examples, and possibly exercises.

- *Conclusion*: summarise what your readers have learned, and encourage them to put their new knowledge into action. Look to the future and describe how their lives will be different now they've read your book.

Transformational memoir

In this category of book you tell your own story of personal transformation, helping your readers to learn from your experience. You can either relate your story chronologically or split it into themes and ideas – both routes are valid. This can be a powerful way of putting across your message, but the mistake many authors make is not to ensure that their story is completely relevant to their readers. By following this top-level outline you'll avoid this trap.

If you're not sure what elements of your story to include, try this exercise. Take a sheet of paper and divide it lengthways. List the main points of your story on the left and the lessons you want to impart on the right. Then draw lines between the two lists to match them up, the result of which will give you a solid starting point for your book outline.

You'll find it helpful to read other transformational memoirs and see how they've created an interesting and useful read, choosing the techniques you find most relevant and incorporating them into your own. Deciding how to tell your story, and weaving the most relevant parts of it into your book as you impart lessons to your readers, isn't an easy process. If you don't enjoy storytelling and find writing narrative hard work, this may not be the best format for you.

- *Introduction*: give your readers an incentive to read your book, with a taster of your story and a preview of what they'll learn from it. How is it relevant to them? What will they gain from it? This is a good place to bring out your personality so your audience starts to get to know you.

- *Chapter 1*: what was your life like when your story began? You could begin before your transformation started (to set the scene), at the beginning of the process, or even at the end.

- *Chapter 2+*: the stages of your story along with the learning points for your readers. One of these chapters should detail your lowest moment and then your turning point – how you realised where you'd been going wrong and what you did to put it right. This is another place you can start your story, because it may be the place your readers are at now.

- *Conclusion*: where you are today and how your readers can gain inspiration from this. An overview of what to do next is also helpful.

Thought-leading, inspirational book

This is an excellent type of book for highlighting the quality and originality of your thinking, and is especially popular with speakers wanting to further their paid speaking careers, or with consultants needing to raise their credibility. It's also highly satisfying to write: How often do we have the chance to expound our ideas, going into them in depth and bringing them to life with examples? This kind of book can also contain an element of 'how-to', as well as incorporating your personal story. Because of this flexibility it's a more difficult category to provide a standard structure for; however, there are still some principles you can apply.

- *Introduction*: your reader has a burning curiosity or concern – that's why they want to learn about your take on it. So empathise with them and explain briefly how you're going to inspire them in your book. Share your credentials (why should they listen to you?), which should include your own experiences in this area.

- *Chapter 1*: go through the background to your topic. Why is it important? And why now? Have you had personal experience with it, and how has that affected your outlook?

- *Chapter 2+*: each element of your subject matter should have its own chapter. You can break it down in various ways: by the different aspects of it that link to your central thesis, by the action you want your readers to take, by chronology, or by importance.

- *Conclusion:* end on a rousing note – this is your final chance to impress the relevance of this subject upon your readers and encourage them to take action (if that's your aim).

Collection of interviews

This is a useful style of book if you enjoy talking to people, especially as it makes compiling your content relatively easy. It also allows you to appear on the radar of, and develop closer relationships with, influencers in your field, which is ideal for promoting your book and building your business profile. However, please don't think that all it involves is transcribing some conversations and putting them in a book – you need to make the topic compelling and meaningful. One drawback of this format is that although it might seem like a good idea to gain your content from others, it does mean you're not the 'star' of your book – this has implications if you want it to build your authority.

An obvious format is to create a new chapter for each interview, but you can have themed chapters instead in which you talk about what you've learned together with examples from various interviewees. For instance, if you've interviewed various finance experts about how to save money, you might want to take a themed approach as many of them would give similar advice. But if you're interviewing people who have different areas of expertise around a central theme, such as medical professionals talking about mental health, then a chapter per interviewee could work well.

- *Introduction*: what will your readers learn from this book – what's in it for them? What problem do they want to solve? And briefly, what are the credentials of the interviewees and how did you come to meet them (there might be an interesting story here)?

- *Chapter 1+*: each interview or theme has its own chapter, with your introduction and summary topping and tailing them.

- *Summary*: make your points clear for your readers, as the nature of interviews means they may have been obscured at various points during the book.

- *Conclusion*: what have your readers learned, and what should they do next?

How to choose

You'll notice these four outline types can overlap: your interview book might contain how-to elements, your how-to guide might contain some of your personal story, and your thought-leading book could include interviews with other thinkers on your topic. So don't feel you have to be rigid with your outline type, just consider what the main thrust of your book will be and use these formats as a guide.

The book outline you choose should be connected to the purpose of your book. What do you want your readers to think, feel, and do by the end of it, and which of these is most important? If you want them to *do* something, a how-to guide might be best. If you're keen for them to *think* something, an inspirational book would work well. And if you're prompting them to *feel* something, a memoir or story-based approach could be the answer.

Are you still stuck? Turn to your bookcase or e-reader and glance through the books you've read recently. Which were most helpful and enjoyable for you? Take a look at how they're structured and you'll find clues as to the kind of book you want to write. You can also think of your readers. What kind of book would they appreciate? You can gain a feel for this from your reader avatar; think about the kind of person they are, when they'll fit the reading of it into their lives, and what you'd like them to do, think, or feel once they've finished it. Which outline would suit them best?

What we've covered

❖ Mind mapping and sticky notes are the two easiest ways to brainstorm your content and create a top-level outline.

❖ There are four main categories of business book, each with its own outline type: self-help or how-to guide, transformational memoir, thought-leading book, and collection of interviews.

❖ Choose your category according to how you can best help your readers and what your topic dictates.

❖ These categories are flexible, and elements from one can merge into another.

Chapter 7

Now flesh things out

Understand what you want to say

I never travel without my diary. One should always have
something sensational to read on the train.

Oscar Wilde

Here's where you get down and dirty with your content.
You know what overall structure you want to follow, so it's
time to roll up your sleeves and work out exactly what you
want to say in each chapter. I can't emphasise enough how
helpful this element of planning is, so please don't skip it.
When I coach people to write their books it's often the area
I meet most resistance with, because by this stage they're
champing at the bit to start writing.

The thing is, I've seen what happens when you don't plot
your points first – the book is *much* harder to create. When
you know what you want to say, it's just a question of

typing it; when you're not sure, you have to keep stopping to think and that's mentally taxing. Another benefit of this is that you avoid the soul-crushing discovery part way through that your content needs to be chopped and changed around, or that you don't have as much material for a particular section as you'd thought. This can be a major demotivator, and is a common reason for giving up.

All you need for now is a set of bullet points for each chapter, not paragraphs of explanation; just enough to order your thoughts so you know what comes next. In fact, it's better if you don't go into too much detail as you want to end up with a two- to three-page document that you can scan at a glance.

How it works

Here's an example of a sample chapter that illustrates the principles of how to structure your content within it. Please don't take it as a rigid template, just use it to make sure you've covered off the key elements of a successful chapter.

- *Set your readers up for what you're about to tell them.* This can be through an attention-grabbing hook: a story, a statistic, a question, a challenge, or anything that prompts your readers to pay attention to what they're about to read (see Chapter 9 for more on this).

- *Introduce the main point.* Tell your readers what you'll be covering in this chapter. What's the point of it? Why is it important? What will they learn?

- *Make your subsidiary points.* These should expand upon your main point; they back it up by going into more depth, providing examples, and looking at the chapter's topic from different angles. You can make use of sub-headings here, especially if your book is an instructional guide. This area forms the bulk of your chapter.

- *Stories and examples.* You should include these at regular places throughout, and they can be as short as a two-line example or as long as several pages. How you incorporate them will be dictated by their importance to the book and the kind of outline it's based on. A memoir, for instance, is effectively a long story in its own right, whereas an interview or how-to book would make use of shorter examples and case studies.

- *Conclusion.* Summarise what you've told your readers and what action you want them to take (if any).

You don't need to make every chapter work in exactly the same way, but your readers will sense a disconnect if one is wildly different from the next. Think of your favourite TV series. Maybe it's a detective drama with the same theme tune each week, opening with a scenic shot followed by some pacy dialogue between new and established characters. Next our trusty detective comes onto the scene, and so on. If you had no idea what to expect when you tuned in you'd be distracted by your uncertainty and would pay less attention to the content. In Pat Flynn's book *Will It Fly?*, for instance, he's consistent with how he applies the same road map to each chapter. He starts with an engaging story to hook in his readers, then goes on to explain what he wants them to learn.

Once you have your points for each chapter in a bulleted list, assign an approximate chapter word count. You can do this by taking your target total for the whole book and breaking it down according to how many chapters you have and how much information you'll impart in each one. Your chapters don't have to be of exactly equal length – that would be neither possible nor desirable – but you should aim to be reasonably consistent for the reasons above.

On the subject of consistency, some people worry that their outline seems a little unbalanced when they compare it to their whole field of expertise. For instance, you may be a speaker who excels in how to hold a stage and put your points across in a memorable way, but may be less experienced in how to create eye-catching visual aids. Your outline would most likely focus on the first two elements and not so much on the third. Is that okay? Absolutely – because your business book is a reflection of *you*, not an imaginary expert who's amazing at everything. Find a way to build your book around your zone of genius and don't worry too much about the areas you're less good at, trusting that someone else will have written the definitive book on those. You may still want to include them (and here's a good place to make use of your industry influencers as contributors) but don't assume you have to present a model image to the world.

How not to turn off 25% of your readers

Did you know that we each have our own preferences for how we learn? This was a revelation to me when I discovered it, and I learned a lot about myself in the process. If your book is aiming to change the way your readers think and behave, you need to cater for each inclination; this might feel like a tall order but it's simple when you understand that there are only four main types.

- *Why:* some of us have to know *why* we're being asked to think differently before we commit ourselves to doing it. Otherwise we can't see the point of it.

- *What:* others of us aren't so bothered by why, but want to know *what* to do. If we're learning something new and aren't told what actions or concepts are involved, we feel discouraged: 'Just tell me what to do and I'll be happy.'

- *How:* then there are those who value being told *how* to do something. For them, it's not enough to know what to do on its own; they feel frustrated and will switch off if they're left to work out the how for themselves.

- *What if?* Finally there are those who, whenever they come across a new concept, are keen to know how it will work in the real world; what could go right and what could go wrong? Theory isn't enough for them, they need real-life examples.

What type are you? I'm a 'why' person, in that if I don't know why I'm doing something I find it difficult to motivate myself to do it. I'm also not a 'how' person and would rather work that element out for myself; that means I become easily bored when explaining the 'how' to others. So if I'm not careful in my writing, I spend a lot of time on 'why' and miss out the 'how' completely – it's my natural bias. Take a moment to work out yours.

You can see how important it is to cater for all four biases in your book, and this relates not just to the whole volume but to each chapter and point you make within it. Start with why what you're about to say is important; explain what your readers should do about it; give them advice on how; and ensure you include some real-world examples or context to put your ideas into. This sounds terribly formulaic but it doesn't have to come across that way. In this book I've done my best to cater for all four learning types, but I don't expect you've noticed it.

Here's a simple example. 'When you're managing someone, they do their best work for you if they know that you care about them as a whole person and not just as a team member [*why*]. Chatting to them about their family and weekend plans is a good way to do that [*what*], but try and keep it casual – you don't want them to think you're prying [*how*]. When I started doing this with my team, I found we trusted each other more and were happier working together [*what if?*].'

Use what you have

Earlier on I mentioned using content you've already created in your book. If you've been sharing your expertise for a while, you'll probably be amazed when you review how much of it there is. Blog posts, presentations, videos, podcast interviews – the list goes on. What have you already created that you could plunder?

You may be wondering how to collate and reference these source materials. It depends on their nature and also your personal preferences. When I sat down to plan the outline for this book, I printed out the last 50 blog posts I'd written and numbered them. Then I noted the main points I'd made in each, alongside the number of the post. This enabled me to compile a list of points for my outline, each with a numbered blog post next to it, which made it easy to reference the material I'd already written. It meant I wasn't starting from scratch, but was making use of my existing intellectual property as well.

You could use index cards, or online clipping and collating tools such as Evernote.[1] It's also helpful to have a way of capturing ideas while you're out and about, such as a notebook or a way of storing ideas in your phone. One of my favourite and low-tech methods is to jot random thoughts on the back of my hand when I'm struck by a flash of genius. This usually happens at the gym (the treadmill is a fabulous idea generator, I find) and the staff are used to me frantically grabbing one of their pens to scribble down

---

[1] Evernote, www.evernote.com/

a memory-jogging word before I forget it. A hand also has the added advantage it will never be lost; as a friend once told me, 'if you lose your hand you're really in trouble'.

A final checklist

You're getting there – well done! Now you know what you need to start writing your book, who it's for, what it's about, and how you're going to make it work for your business. Not bad going, and if you've done everything I've suggested you'll be streets ahead of the majority of business authors who plunge straight into the writing. You should also be able to tick each of these statements:

☐ You know what you want your book to achieve for your readers, yourself, and your business

☐ You understand who it's for and can describe a sample person from that readership in depth

☐ You've planned a book your readers want, not just need

☐ Your book is based on a message that aligns with your professional expertise

☐ Your book will be irresistible to your readers because it answers a key question that's relevant to them

☐ You can summarise what your book will deliver for your readers in one sentence

☐ You have some idea how you're going to promote it when it's finished

Before you go any further, put your outline and chapter plan in writing. You can find a handy template at https://marketingtwentyone.co.uk/plan. Taking the time to do that now will increase your chances of creating the book that puts you in the spotlight.

What we've covered

* ❖ It's vital to plan your points within each chapter before you start writing – this will save you much time and effort.

* ❖ Aim for broad consistency in format and length for each chapter.

* ❖ Ensure you've covered off why, what, how, and what if? for each chapter and every point within it.

* ❖ Carry out a final check on your book plan before you proceed.

II
WRITE

Chapter 8

Writing clearly

How to make yourself understood

Making the simple complicated is commonplace; making the complicated simple, awesomely simple, that's creativity.
Charles Mingus, jazz musician

When I was 22, I landed a second interview for a job on a prestigious management training scheme. I was eager to impress – jobs with prospects were scarce at the time and I didn't want to blow one of my few chances so far. So I donned my best (actually my only) suit and tried to look as serious and professional as I could. My interviewer was a genial man in his fifties with the air of someone who'd seen every mistake in business there is to make. After a few exploratory questions he smiled and asked, 'So Ginny, tell me. What do you think is more important for a manager: to be liked or to be respected?' This was a good question and

I had my answer ready. 'Oh, respected, for sure', I replied. After all, I thought, if a manager is only *liked* people will run rings around them, right?

Wrong. 'You made the same mistake as all the other candidates', he said, as kindly as possible given he was delivering a killer blow. 'Think about it. Have you ever respected someone you didn't *like*? I mean, why would you want to listen to them? Why would you trust them?'

He was right, dammit. Because with rare exceptions, if we're to pay attention to the views of someone who we don't know well, we first need to be sure that they have our best interests at heart. And when we pick up a book we're more likely to trust the author if we develop a rapport with them. A key way to generate these feelings of trust in our readers is to write clearly and persuasively for them; clarity shows we're respectful of their time and attention, and persuasiveness is how we tap into their emotions.

(In case you're wondering, I still got the job.)

Generating trust is, as we've seen, a key factor in persuasion. But there's no use getting your readers on your side if they don't understand what you're telling them in the first place, which is why clarity is the first nut to crack. I'll cover writing clearly in this chapter and persuasively in the next.

Writing for understanding has three elements, and as you'd expect with anything to do with clarity they come in a linear order.

1. Create a logical overall structure (which you've already done in Chapter 6).

2. Plot your points so they work together (some of which you did in Chapter 7 but will refine here).

3. Write them so they're easy to understand (which I'll also cover here).

Refine the order of your points

As any clothes stylist will tell you, a fabulous end result is reliant on sound underpinning and it's the same with books. Previously you learned how to create a list of the points you want to make in each chapter. When you've done this, cast your eye over the order they're in. At what point are you 'joining' your readers? Each chapter and sub-section of your book should start by meeting them during the conversation they're *already having* with themselves, not at the point at which you assume they're starting. This is the best way to make your message irresistible – you're giving people what they're looking for, not only what you think they should have.

To gain a sense of this, picture your readers ambling along a familiar country path. The scenery is well known to them, and each twist and turn leads to a spot they've visited before. But when they walk around a corner they find themselves standing before a wide open vista (it might even be a cliff edge). The knowledge they've used to reach this far won't help them now, so it's up to you to make your entrance and give them the directions they need.

Your next task is to arrange the points that follow from there so they work naturally with each other. You're aiming to give your readers the next piece of information they need in order to grasp your thought trajectory. One way of doing this is to think, 'If I were my readers, what would I want to know next, and next, and next?' Then, when you've created an order, imagine you were to hop in a helicopter and hover over your list of points. What would you see? A series of landmarks relating to one another in a harmonious way as a river leads to the sea, or a hodgepodge of elements that don't work together? Because every nonfiction book has the aim of convincing its readers about something, which means it's in the business of persuasion. And to be persuasive your arguments need to make sense.

When your points are in the right order, start writing. Just say what you think about each mini-topic without worrying (at this stage) about whether it's well crafted or not. Your aim right now is only to put words on the page. Once you've written the first draft of a whole chapter you may feel the need to do some moving around – in fact you probably will. There's something about the act of writing that clarifies the thinking, and it can seem obvious now that x should come after y and not before, or should even migrate into a different chapter. Planning can get you so far, but it's never the whole story.

Write for understanding

I always think journalists have an inbuilt advantage when it comes to clear writing, because they're trained to put their facts across without their readers having to try hard to understand. In fact you can learn a lot from them by casting a critical eye over the next media piece you read, whether it be a news article or in-depth interview. But how can the rest of us make the words we write easy to absorb? Here are some key points to bear in mind when you want to make yourself clear.

Beware of the curse of knowledge

I watched a hilarious video recently, in which two teenage boys were given the challenge of making a call using an old-fashioned dial-up (or rotary) telephone.[1] I remember as a teenager sitting in my family hallway on one of those phones, tethered to the wall by a curly wire. So what happened in the experiment? First of all, the boys didn't realise they needed to pick up the receiver *before* they dialled the number (well, why would they?). Then they struggled to move the numbers on the dial, having to learn from scratch how to turn and release it. They gamely battled on, but after several minutes of experimentation were still not able to complete the task.

This is a perfect example of the curse of knowledge. When you've done something a zillion times it's difficult to imagine what it's like for someone who's new to it. Depending on the level of your readers' expertise, you have to take a sizeable step back from your topic and imagine what you would need to be told if you were them. If you leave gaps, you'll confuse them. The best way to test whether you've got it right is to ask a few people in your target readership if they can understand what you've written. You'll be surprised at what you might have missed out.

---

[1] '17 Year Olds Dial a Rotary Phone', *Interesting Engineering*, www.interestingengineering.com/video/watch-two-teenagers-try-to-dial-a-number-on-an-ancient-rotary-phone

Stay focused

For every paragraph, you should be able to say what the purpose of it is. Why have it at all? And why have it *there*? Digressing and rambling is the easiest way to confuse and bore your readers. When you catch yourself doing this give yourself a pat on the back because you've just realised something vital: you don't fully understand what you're trying to say. That's okay, we all do it – just revisit your thoughts and ask yourself if they're needed at all. If they are, are they in the right place?

If you're concerned you're not focused enough, try going through your draft chapter and jotting down the point you're making for each paragraph in the order you've written them in. Then read them through as bullets on their own and decide if they're in a sensible sequence. It's a fantastic way of making sure the skeleton of your content hangs together as it should.

Use plain English

I'm not going to give you a grammar lesson as that would be dull, but please take care not to bamboozle your readers with unwieldy sentences and paragraphs. I pity the poor souls who were supposed to take action on this letter to a newspaper I saw recently:

> Although there is a clear 'Stop' sign posted
> for bikers and pedestrians, and they're not
> supposed to cross until the ramp is clear, if a
> motorist is coming around a curve and sees
> a person or a biker approaching the ramp,
> instinct may kick in, causing the motorist

to swerve, stop, or react negatively in order
to avoid the possibility of hitting him,
which unfortunately may cause another
collision altogether.

My eyes were going around in circles as I tried to mentally circumnavigate this sentence.

If grammar and word flow isn't your strength, don't worry. A good copy editor or even a ghostwriter will be able to help you here – just factor this into your planning and budgeting for now and we'll cover it later on.

Be sparse

As silence is a part of music, so white space is an essential element of writing – it gives it shape and rhythm. So help your text to breathe by breaking it up with sub-headings, lists, and paragraphs, and don't expect your readers to wade through reams of dense text. The space around your words is something they won't notice; they'll just have a feeling of ease as they read, which makes it likely they'll enjoy and understand your book.

Punctuate for effect

To use another music analogy, punctuation and sentence length are to writing what a conductor's baton is to performance. Having nothing but short, punchy sentences feels aggressive and monotonous. Having all long, flowery ones feels a bit like wading through treacle. But mix them up in the right way and you create the perfect recipe for giving emphasis to the relevant things. Nothing draws attention better than a sudden change of tempo, so if you have a forceful point to make write it in a short sentence with no embellishment. If you want to encourage your readers to consider a more complex argument, make use of clauses, semi-colons, and commas.

Now you understand how to write clearly, it's time to take your words and wave a magic wand over them. You're about to learn the fascinating art of persuasive writing, a skill that will transform your ability to communicate in any medium and raise the level of your influence further than you could imagine.

What we've covered

- ❖ Writing clearly is a key element of bringing your readers over to your way of thinking.
- ❖ Ensure your points are in an order that makes sense to your readers, not only to you.
- ❖ Write so your readers can understand you by giving the right amount of explanation, using clear language, and thinking about how you structure your sentences.

Chapter 9

Writing persuasively

How to win over your readers

Metaphors be with you.
Professor Harvey Mindess, author and psychologist

I once heard a high-level diplomat describe diplomacy as 'the art of letting other people have your way'. The same can be said of persuasion, and if you're a speaker, coach, or thought-leader whose work revolves around helping people to move from one place to another, you'll be familiar with its power. You'll understand that it doesn't happen because you've *told* someone they should do something, but because you've laid a path for them they can't help but follow. When you know how to do this in your writing your book will become a force for change.

Make an introduction

The introduction is often the chapter people find hardest to create, and yet it's the most important because it's the one that will make or break your readers' decision as to whether to buy and read your book. Once they've checked out your title, cover, and blurb, they'll flick (or scroll) through the first few pages to see if you're the kind of person they want to learn from. For reasons I'll explain in a moment, it's not a great idea to write your introduction before the rest of your book. But from my experience of working with coaching clients I know that's what you might be intending to do, so I'll cover how to write a compelling introduction now.

When was the last time you read the first paragraph of a book and thought to yourself, 'Hmm, this looks pretty tedious but I bet it contains some useful information. I'll buy it and make myself read it from cover to cover, even if it kills me.' I'm guessing never, which brings me to the central purpose of an introduction: it's to capture your readers' interest and earn their trust. You want to draw them in and convince them that their lives won't be the same if they don't buy and read your book right now. So many authors use their introduction as a place to expound on their book's theme, and why and how they wrote it; these are not the factors that will persuade people to invest time and money in it. Your potential readers frankly don't care what drove you to spend three years creating your magnum opus, at least not until you've convinced them they're going to get something valuable out of it.

So why is a book's introduction the final chapter you should write? Because you're setting the book's scene for your readers, and it's tricky to do this before you've written the rest of it. Also, your writing style will improve as you write everything else, and given the introduction is the most important chapter to do well it makes sense to draft it last.

How do you write an introduction so it persuades people to buy your book? Here's a helpful framework:

1. Tell your readers in your first few lines what the book's about. In other words, what problem you'll be solving or what subject you'll be exploring. They want to know up front whether it's of interest to them.

2. Empathise with your readers, showing you understand their pain or curiosity; the phrase 'people don't care what you know until they know that you care' is spot on here. At the same time make it clear you're familiar with who your target readers are, because they need to feel confident this book is for them. You should be happy for the 'wrong' readers to leave you at this point.

3. Briefly present your solution or explanation. This is the 'gold' in your book.

4. Explain your credibility: What makes you qualified to write about this topic?

5. Tell your readers what they'll get out of the book: advice, information, entertainment, or knowledge. Be concrete and make a big promise.

6. Encourage them to read on now – create a sense of urgency.

Your introduction can also be a good place to tell a relevant story, thereby creating interest and the desire to read on. It's not usually the place to launch into your full life history, though – save that for later if you need it.

Keep 'em hooked

The attention and trust you earn in your introduction isn't a one-off thing – you have to keep earning it in every subsequent chapter you write. Think of yourself as a supermarket with a loyalty card scheme, giving rewards to your consumers not just on their first visit but every time they return. Winning this repeat business means being persuasive. There are two elements to this: using the *way you write* to win people over, and creating *interesting content* so they want to read on.

The good news is, there's only one thing you need to do if you want to be a persuasive writer, and that's to put yourself in your readers' shoes. Ask yourself if what you're saying is relevant, and if you're making a difference to the way they feel. Because without a shift in emotions, there's no change at all. Your mission as a business book writer is usually to inspire your readers to *do* something different, and to do that they have to *feel* different.

So sensing how your readers think and feel is key, but there are a few other tips and tricks for writing persuasively that you'll love.

Start strong

The end of one chapter and the start of another create a natural pause point at which your readers will ask themselves if they want to carry on. So each time you begin a new chapter of your book, you're expecting people to make a decision. There's a simple strategy canny business book authors use to make their books unputdownable (if that's a word), which is to start each chapter with a hook. This can be a story, a surprising statistic, a controversial fact, a provocative question – anything that piques readers' interest and prompts them to continue. Once they're a page into your chapter, they're usually yours for the duration.

Be specific

People are happier to remember and trust the specific than the general; when your readers trust you, your book will have a profound effect on them. This means specific elements such as quotes, statistics, facts, and examples automatically make your writing more persuasive.

Being specific also means being concrete, which in writing terms involves you describing things in a way your readers can experience through their senses rather than their rational minds. Everyday examples are 'sign on the dotted line' instead of 'agree the contract', or 'I smell a rat' instead of 'there's something wrong'. As Lisa Cron explains in her book *Wired for Story:* 'If you can't picture it, it's general. If you can see it, it's specific.'[1]

---

[1] Lisa Cron, *Wired for Story*, Ten Speed Press, 2012.

One of my favourite ways to show the power of specificity is to look at how comedians do it. Comedy actors are masters and mistresses of the specific comment, because they know it drives a strong reaction. The late Victoria Wood is my go-to example; her writing was funny for many reasons, but one of them was because she was so particular with her details. For her this made her audiences laugh, but for you it might result in your readers feeling touched, understood, impressed, or moved. I can't resist giving you some examples:

- 'Foreplay is like beefburgers – three minutes on each side' (it's the 'three minutes' that makes me laugh, along with the visual image of burgers being flipped).

- 'You know that building in London where all the windows blew out? That wasn't a bomb, it was fifty-six pre-menstrual women the day the chocolate machine broke down' (it had to be fifty-six).

- 'I once found myself in bed with a man who was a real do-it-yourself enthusiast... He ripped off all his clothes and said, "What would you like me to do?" I said, "Well, really I'd like you to fix my overflow and re-point my brickwork"' (if she'd just said 'do some jobs around the house' it wouldn't have been half as funny).

For Victoria it was never just a biscuit, it was a macaroon; it was never just a magazine, it was a *Woman's Weekly*; and it was never just DIY, it was lagging the pipes.

So try to avoid too many generalised statements such as 'By improving your communication skills your team will deliver more effectively' – that's the kind of stuff readers gloss over. Instead, give an example of a client who raised their revenue by a certain percentage, or a statistic that backs up your argument. You could even tell the story of someone who did something particular to improve their communication skills and achieved a result. You'll be memorable, and your readers will believe you because you've made what you're saying real to them.

Use metaphors and images

There's a book sitting on my bookshelf: *The Tall Lady With The Iceberg* by Anne Miller (how's that for a memorable title?).[2] Appropriately, the book is filled with reasons why you should use metaphors, similes, and other imagery in your writing and (in her case) your presentations and speaking too. There's often no better way of putting across a complex point clearly and memorably than to use an analogy to describe it; think of it as doing the heavy lifting for your ideas.

In addition, helping your readers to visualise something instead of giving them an abstract explanation is easier on their brains, and the less effort they have to put into absorbing what you write the more likely they are to grasp what you're telling them. As Mardy Grothe said in another brilliant book about metaphors, *I Never Metaphor I Didn't*

---

[2] Anne Miller, *The Tall Lady With The Iceberg*, Chiron Associates, 2012.

Like,[3] 'When people create metaphors, they find similarities between things that, on the surface, are dissimilar. A good metaphor is like a bridge that links to territories that have been separated by a body of water or a deep canyon. Once the bridge is connected, people can travel freely back and forth.'

You might feel daunted by creating images for your writing because it can be hard to conjure up appropriate ones, so here's a way of making it easier. Let's look at how you could choose a metaphor for describing the challenges of running a group coaching session.

1. List the standout features of a group coaching session. They could include the following:

    *   crowd control;

    *   feeling you have to be all things to all people;

    *   being 'on show' for your audience.

2. Think about other scenarios that share similar features to each of the above in turn. For instance:

    *   being a classroom teacher keeping all the students in check;

    *   being a parent who feels they have to spread their time equally between their children;

    *   being an actor on stage.

3. Consider which of these is most appropriate to your features by challenging yourself on the detail:

---

[3] Mardy Grothe, *I Never Metaphor I Didn't Like*, HarperCollins, 2008.

- being a teacher is similar but that implies the coach is telling their clients what to do, which isn't how coaching works;

- being a parent has similarities with running a group coaching session because of the caring nature of the role, but it's a lifelong commitment rather than a one-off;

- being an actor resonates somewhat, but implies a performance for the audience rather than a deep involvement.

Each of these analogies has a drawback, but you could take the parenting analogy and tweak it so it's relevant for a specific occasion, such as a father torn between attending his daughter's school play and his son's football match. This could work as it's a relatable scenario: 'Running a group coaching session can feel like being a dad who's torn between attending his daughter's school play and his son's football match. You worry that choosing one person to give your attention to leads to others feeling left out.'

Write like you mean it

While we're on the subject of trust, there's another way to bring your readers into your world willingly and that's to write like you mean it. There are many ways of doing this, which we'll explore here.

Write like 'you'

If your book reads like the author has stepped into the shoes of another writer, it comes across as false. None of us does this on purpose, but it's an easy slip to make. The default option when we don't feel too confident about our writing style is to unconsciously copy some other writer we admire, or to revert back to the academic essays we wrote at school or college. However, there's a vital difference between our teachers and our readers: our teachers were paid to read our musings and our readers are not.

'Finding your voice' is something you hear writers talk about, but what does it mean? It's an elusive concept, but to me it's about sounding like you're you but in the context of a book. It's not the 'you' your friends would find in the local coffee shop, nor is it the 'you' your kids would recognise when you tuck them in at night. It's not even the 'you' your email recipients or Facebook friends would know. It's the 'you' that uses the words that come naturally, while writing in a semi-formal way. Another way of thinking about it is to work out what it's *not*. It's not you being a lecturer or a teacher, nor is it you using long words and complicated sentences because you think it makes you seem important. Believe me, your ideas are noteworthy enough without any hype.

So how do you write like you? One way is to consciously abandon the desire to impress. Just put your words down as if you were talking to someone you know, and go for it. You can also record yourself speaking and have it transcribed (or use dictation software that does the transcribing for you); once you've tidied it up and formalised it you have your writing voice right there. It's amazing what a difference it makes when your readers feel like you're speaking to them personally rather than to a hall of students.

Write to your readers

Using the passive voice is an easy trap to fall into, so it's worth keeping a wary eye out for it. The passive voice is when, instead of using an active verb ('You can hold workshops to attract clients') you use a passive way of saying the same thing ('Workshops to attract clients can be held'). It's the kind of writing you'll often find in academic texts and in books by authors who don't understand what a distancing effect it creates. If you don't want to come across as a crusty professor, I advise you to avoid it.

Take this example: 'The question more accurately put is, "Is leadership in crisis?"' It's hard to know where this author is coming from, and even harder to care. Is he talking to us (the readers) or to himself? And why does he have to sound like he's standing at a lectern? He's leaving us feeling as if we're standing on our own when we want him to be beside us, his arm around our shoulders, talking to us in an encouraging way. Maybe he could have re-phrased it thus: 'Can I ask you: Is leadership in crisis?' Now he's speaking directly to us, and we feel interested and engaged.

Be personal

Do you have the feeling as you're writing that you've lost sight of your ideal reader? Clues to this are not being sure whether you should include something, or finding yourself imagining an amorphous crowd of readers rather than just one. Try conjuring that target reader back into your mind and addressing all your words to that one person. You'll be pleased at how much more direct, warm, and interested you sound (as well as your content being relevant and interesting).

Be substantial

Does your book have enough substance to it? I don't mean a sufficient number of words or pages, but enough heft to its arguments? Flimsy writing can creep up on you when you least expect it, such as when you find yourself making generalisations and putting your points across without any evidence to back them up. Ask yourself if you could include any of the following to make your key points more credible:

- a personal story or case study;
- a metaphor that adds clarity and interest;
- statistics and facts that back up what you're saying;
- illustrations and diagrams, if they add value; and
- examples of how other people have done what you're suggesting.

Avoid crutch words

When we speak we use lots of filler and generic words like 'actually' and 'really', and that's fine. But in your writing you want to do away with them as much as you can, because they take attention away from your meaning and can even make you sound evasive and unsure. They're words such as:

- really
- actually

- probably
- quite
- truly
- very
- anyway
- literally
- almost
- all
- great
- good
- bad
- in my opinion (the whole book is your opinion)

These crutch words hobble your writing rather than propping it up, because they're either bland, meaningless, or so common as to have become redundant. When you're next tempted to write 'in my opinion, this is actually a great way to get good at coaching', try and find more specific word choices that will punch through powerfully. How about: 'this is the most effective way to become a fully-booked coach'. Which option sounds most persuasive to you?

Avoid clichés like the plague

Ah, clichés – so effortless to write, so easy to hate. They're like a comfy sofa, ready to catch you as a fallback when you're tired and in a rush. There's no problem with using them occasionally, but your writing will be a more interesting read if you make a conscious effort to banish them. See if you can do a cliché-spotting session while you edit your book.

Treat acronyms with care (TAWC)

Acronyms can be helpful in clarifying a theme or concept, but they come with a health warning. (If you're not sure what they are, they're abbreviations formed from the initial letters of words, such as NASA.) Much beloved by creators of frameworks and systems, they have the benefit of making processes memorable and easy to understand. But – and there's a big but – they're only worth using if they make things easy for you and your readers. I've coached authors who've tied themselves in knots trying to create acronyms for their book structures, and it's caused them all sorts of difficulties when the letters they want to use don't fit exactly with what they want to say, or aren't in the right order.

I'm reminded of a conversation I had years ago with my husband when we were in the process of organising our wedding. It was only a couple of weeks to go until the big day, and I found myself inexplicably stressed about what colour the table napkins were going to be. 'Now I'm worrying about the napkins', I said to him. 'Just tell me to stop it.' He looked up and calmly replied with his best dry humour: 'Yeah. Everyone's going to come away from our wedding saying, "Great day, it was so wonderful seeing them get married. Shame about the *napkins*!"'

It was exactly what I needed to hear. In the same way, no one is going to read your book and say, 'Great read, it was so enlightening. Shame there wasn't an *acronym*.' If it's not there they won't miss it, so give yourself a break and scrap the whole notion if it's driving you mad.

Ditch the adverbs

As Stephen King said in his book *On Writing*: 'The road to hell is paved with adverbs.'[4] But your teacher always taught you to use them to colour up your writing, right? I'm sure they did and there's no need to eliminate them altogether, but consider this: adverbs are often a way of avoiding coming up with a stronger verb in the first place, which means they can become yet another filler. For example, 'He walked onto the stage nervously' would be more powerful if it became, 'He edged onto the stage' – it's more evocative and visual, and you've stripped out an unnecessary word to boot.

Adverbs tend to be used as padding, too: 'it was entirely impractical'. Do we need the 'entirely'? Is it contributing anything useful? If not, lose it.

Don't be a repeater

We all have our favourite words and boy do we love to use them again, and again, and again. I know one of mine is 'great', which is a weak word too – ugh! But I'm aware of it and try not to use it without good reason. That's why it's helpful to have a copy editor read through your manuscript, as their objective eye will spot the guilty repetitions more easily than yours can.

---

[4] Stephen King, *On Writing: A Memoir of the Craft*, Hodder Paperbacks, 2012.

Harness the power of stories

When Facebook CEO Sheryl Sandberg gave her famous 2010 TED Talk, 'Why we have too few women leaders', she'd originally planned to cram it with facts and figures. Luckily for her audience, she confided in a friend shortly before taking to the stage. Sheryl told her that her daughter had been so upset to see Mummy fly off to yet another conference, she'd clung to her leg as she was leaving for the airport. This was the guilt every mother lives with, Sheryl said. Her friend persuaded her to include this story in her talk and it made a huge difference to the level of emotional connection she gained with her audience.[5]

More often than not, the inclusion of stories in a business book is the element that turns it from good to outstanding. In fact, some business books (also called 'business parables') are stories from beginning to end; *The Goal* by Eliyahu Goldratt is a brilliant example – it manages to make manufacturing process improvement both fascinating and easy to understand.[6]

Why are stories so powerful?

They create memorability

Think of the nonfiction books you've read that included plenty of stories – I bet you can remember them better

---

[5] 'Why We Have Too Few Women Leaders', *TED*, www.ted.com/talks/sheryl_sandberg_why_we_have_too_few_women_leaders?language=en

[6] Eliyahu M. Goldratt, *The Goal: A Process of Ongoing Improvement*, Routledge, 2004.

than the facts you learned. That's because, ever since our early ancestors sat around the camp fire telling their cave-mates about the dangers and triumphs of their day, we've been programmed to pay attention to stories. We can't help wanting to know what comes next. Did the annoying cave guy from down the valley lose his fight with the woolly mammoth and get his just desserts, or did the mammoth end up becoming said dessert? If you want your readers to remember what you tell them, use stories to illustrate your points.

They add breathability

Stories bring life and excitement to your book. Not only do they break up your descriptions by adding variety, but by taking your audience into a different world they inject a shot of imagination. When you switch between fact and fiction, this stimulates your readers' brains to react in different ways. And the more our minds are engaged with a book, the more likely we are to keep reading.

They add credibility

If you want to convince your audience you're the right person to help them, a personal story reveals a lot more about you than dry facts and figures or even plain advice. When you recount how you helped someone in the context of your work, your readers will be likely to trust whatever else you say.

They're scientifically proven to work

Researchers at Princeton University discovered a remarkable thing that happens when you hear a story.[7] Personal stories cause the brains of both storyteller and listener to exhibit what they call 'brain to brain coupling'. In other words, telling personal stories puts you in sync with your readers.

So stories are important – in fact they're vital for any business book. They're also the element that can stump business writers the most. 'Do I have any stories? What stories should I use? And how should I tell them?' Remember, a story doesn't have to be something from the world around you – it can be a case study or an example of someone you've helped. It's simply a tale that has a beginning, middle, and end. You can generate stories by thinking back to the interactions you've had with people (personal or professional), scanning your testimonials and contact list for memory-joggers, and asking your clients. Also – and this is vital – if a fantastic story idea pops into your head while you're out and about, make a note of it. I have a document I put all my story ideas into, along with thoughts on what points they could illustrate.

How to tell a story

This warrants a book in its own right, and indeed there are many written on this theme. For your purpose as a business book writer, I'd recommend *The Storytelling Toolkit* by

---

[7] Carmine Gallo, 'How Sheryl Sandberg's Last Minute Addition to Her TED Talk Sparked a Movement', *Forbes*, 28 February 2014.

Lynda McDaniel and Virginia McCullough. In it they explain the six steps to a successful story:[8]

- *A hook.* This draws your readers' attention to the story you're about to tell. What's in it for them? Why would they want to read on? You need something juicy to tempt them in.

- *Set the scene.* What's the context for your tale? Bring it to life with sensory details, either in a 'once upon a time' sort of way, or by plunging your readers into the middle of the situation.

- *Conflict and complications.* What's the pain at the centre of your story? What are your main characters struggling to overcome?

- *Development.* Explain how the situation progresses, including who does what.

- *Resolution.* How does it end? Satisfy your readers' curiosity by being clear on the conclusion.

- *Call to action.* This is where a business book story is different to a novel. What learning can your readers take from the story? Explain what you'd like them to do, think, or feel as a result of reading it.

So you've learned how to write a clear and persuasive book – no mean feat! But what happens when you start writing it? This is what we'll explore next.

---

[8] Lynda McDaniel and Virginia McCullough, *The Storytelling Toolkit*, E-book.

What we've covered

❖ Writing persuasively is an essential part of retaining your readers' attention and building their trust.

❖ The purpose of your book's introduction is to encourage people to buy and read it.

❖ After your introduction, your task is to keep your readers turning the pages, chapter after chapter.

❖ Keeping your readers on your side involves writing directly and honestly.

❖ Include stories throughout your book to aid memorability, breathability, and credibility to what you say.

Chapter 10

Insider tips for easier writing

How to smooth the journey

There are just three rules for writing, but nobody knows what they are.
Somerset Maugham, bestselling author

You've been putting it off for days. Okay, weeks. Well, a couple of months actually – no make that three. But today a client cancelled their session so you have two hours to spare. Today is the day you'll write the next chapter of your book. But wait a minute. Did you forget to lock the back door when you came in? How about your car? And what's that strange noise outside? You'd better check.

They're all fine, so now it's time to write. Right now. No more stalling, just begin.

You put a few lines down; they're a start. Hang on, though, is this the best you can do? Nope, hit the delete key and start again. Now you have no lines. 'I must be clueless, lazy, an amateur', you think. 'Why did I ever think I could write a book? I should do myself a favour and give up now.'

All authors feel this way – even the top-selling ones. It's called resistance. French writer Victor Hugo couldn't get down to *The Hunchback of Notre Dame* without locking himself inside his house with nothing to wear but a full-length shawl (for some reason this made him more productive). Novelist Graham Greene didn't feel able to write until he'd seen certain numbers by accident; he'd wait by the side of the road until they appeared on passing licence plates. Your manifestations of resistance might be more prosaic, but they're no less obstructive.

- It's the wrong time of day. Or week. Or something.
- You need time to find the perfect metaphor for that point.
- You decamp to your local coffee shop for a latte and some productive writing. But you don't get anything done due to the loud music, free wifi, and 15 screaming babies from the local parents' group.
- Ping! A vital email arrives.
- Your cat just sat on your keyboard (you're getting desperate now).

Again: you're not alone. While writing this book my email inbox has never been so clear, my accounts so up to date, and my social media so well scanned. Let's face it, writing is hard work because it involves thinking, and thinking is challenging. It also means communicating with clarity, creativity, and persuasiveness – that's no picnic either.

Your highest hurdles

When I ask myself why it can be so hard to write I don't have all the answers, but from talking to experts on how our minds work and listening to the problems my clients have, I've picked up some helpful answers that point the way to solutions.

Recognise that fear is the mother of resistance

As authors, our biggest dread is of rejection: by publishers, readers, and our peers. This is linked to the terror of being 'found out': we irrationally believe that once people read our books we'll be exposed for knowing little of value. Transformative coach Michael Neill points out something interesting about fear, which is that it's not what we're really feeling in situations like this. True fear is when we think we're going to die, which is something I hope a book could never bring about! What we're really experiencing is worry, which is a different thing entirely. Worry is always going to be part of life's journey, and it never achieved anything; the trick is to see it as not telling us anything important about what might happen in reality.

Another way to look at this is not to care that you feel afraid. This seems almost impossible to do, but why should it be? What matters is that you enjoy writing your book, throwing yourself into the experience wholeheartedly. You could think of it as background chatter in a restaurant while you have a delicious meal with a friend; it's there, but it doesn't interfere with the main event.

Fear can also be caused by the belief that completing your book is somehow not possible. Pictured in the round, we can see the end day when our book is finished and believe it can be done. But sit us down in front of a keyboard, and somehow that faith is shaken. The key to fostering our sense of self-belief isn't to try and talk ourselves out of it (because that always works, right?), but to acknowledge that failure is a possibility, as is success. You've never written a book before, but so what? It doesn't mean you can't do it. You don't know until you try so why not give yourself a chance?

Own your motive

If you're struggling to get started, ask yourself if you truly want to write this book or if you're just doing it because it seems like a good idea. If it's the latter you'll find it hard to finish it – and let's not go into what quality it will be. If writing a book isn't what you feel called to do, there are other paths you can take to achieve your aims.

But consider this as well. What would it be like to see the process of writing your book as fascinating and inspiring, instead of a chore? I talked earlier about how much you can learn about your expertise by writing a book, and how this can be worth the effort even if you were not to publish it. When you think about it like this, writing feels more like being on a bike and coasting downhill instead of peddling furiously upwards; you'll reach your destination far more quickly and easily when you enjoy the ride.

Learn the theory of relativity

Lack of time is the number one reason people give me for why they haven't written their book. It was the same reason I used for years, too. It's funny, because time can appear fixed to us – we all know there are 24 hours in the day. But take a step back and it becomes more fluid. As Shakespeare said in *As You Like It*, 'Time travels in diverse paces with diverse persons.' Think of when you have ten things to do before a presentation – an hour flies by. But when you're waiting for a train on a chilly platform it drags for ages. This helps us to see time as a relative concept.

We tend to find time in our lives for what we most want to do. I bet when the next episode of your favourite TV series comes on you carve out an hour to watch it, so consider your motivation along with a more fluid attitude towards time – it can be a magical combination. Also, bear in mind there's no set number of months for how long it should take to write your book. If you're feeling overwhelmed at any point, it might be you've just not done a terribly good job of predicting how long the process will be. I sometimes hear people boast about how quickly they wrote their book but my question to myself is always, 'So what?'

Recognise your achievement

Writing a book isn't a walk in the park. By some miracle you may find it so, and if you do you have my admiration and envy, but for the rest of the world it's a long-term effort. Some people think they can cobble together a heap of blog posts or interview transcripts and voilà – a book will emerge fully formed. Sadly this is never the case.

The reason being a business author is such a mark of authority is because you've proved you have the intellectual grasp of your subject, along with the sticking power, to write a whole book about it – a book that entertains, educates, and enlightens your readers. The truth is, there are no shortcuts to writing a book of substance so please don't try. Once you've acknowledged the challenging, fascinating, frustrating, time-consuming, exhausting, and rewarding nature of the beast, you'll be one step nearer to rekindling your energy and commitment. You need a fire in your belly to complete your book. It's got to matter to you.

Being practical for a moment

Hopefully these pointers will help you to see your difficulties as being the mirages they really are. But what if you want some more practical ways of jumping over these hurdles? A whole heap of these are coming right up.

Don't write a book

Seriously. How about, instead of writing a book right now, creating a series of blog posts or a talk you're giving next week? As long as it's relevant to your big message it can fulfil a dual purpose by giving you the content you need today, as well as eventually contributing to your book. When you have a deadline it's easier to get things done, so if you need a post for your e-newsletter this week you can make sure it's on a topic that can be easily fitted into one of your chapters. Not only will this help you write with less pain, it also ensures it's integrated into your business communications.

Speak your book into the world

In *Big Magic,* Elizabeth Gilbert recounts how the speaker and researcher Brené Brown switched from being a 'martyr' to her book to being a 'trickster'. This meant finding the easiest and most inspirational way for her to write, instead of assuming it had to be a struggle. For Brené this was by speaking her book. She asked a couple of colleagues to take notes while she told them what she wanted to say. Every so often she'd grab their notes and write the book using them as a guide, thereby also capturing her natural voice; she was delighted with how effective it was.

Writing isn't a natural process. It was something you were taught to do at school, but that can make it all the more difficult; I don't know about you, but I can visualise my teacher's red pen as soon as my first draft appears on the page. Also you're not used to writing at length, so your mental muscles feel out of condition; it shouldn't be a surprise when you don't sprint out of the starting block like an Olympic athlete who's been training for years.

This is why some authors prefer to talk their book into the world rather than writing it, especially if they speak for a living, either as a professional speaker or as a coach. Ask yourself if, when you have a difficult decision to make, you like to do it by talking it through. And do you tend to think aloud? If you're a 'talker' you'd probably answer yes.[1]

If you're thinking of talking out your book, have your outline pinned down before you begin. It's even more important to know what points you want to make than if you're writing it, otherwise you could meander off track. Use a recording device of your choice, with the ability to export the resulting file into a format you can save onto your desktop or email to your transcriber. Then imagine your target reader is sitting across from you, eager to hear what you have to say, and speak to them as if they were there. Another way of doing this is to ask a trusted friend or colleague to interview you, using your outline as a guide for their questions.

Afterwards you need to have your recordings transcribed. You can find cost-effective transcribers online; alternatively you could invest in automated transcription software such as Dragon Naturally Speaking, which has the advantage of being cheaper in the long run (although there is a learning curve). Once you have a transcription, treat it as the raw material for your book; this is my method when I ghostwrite my clients' books. Instead of a blank page you have words down already – so much easier. It's not the finished article by any means, but it's a useful starting point. You may find yourself moving chunks of text from one place to another, deleting passages, combining others,

---

[1] For a step-by-step guide, see Joanna Penn, 'How to Speak Your Book', *The Creative Penn*, www.thecreativepenn.com/how-to-dictate-your-book/

and re-writing entire sections; that's okay, because it's still quicker and less daunting than writing from scratch. Useful guides to this process are in 'Further resources' at the end of this book.

Go with the grain

Despite the fact that writing by keyboard rather than by hand is the norm, the creation of words can feel like a no-going-back moment. This doesn't make sense. Feel free to create what Anne Lamott, in her wonderful book on writing *Bird by Bird*, calls 'shitty first drafts'. What a glorious phrase. In fact I love it so much I'm going for the full quote:

> Almost all good writing begins with terrible first efforts. You need to start somewhere. Start by getting something – anything – down on paper. What I've learned to do when I sit down to work on a shitty first draft is to quiet the voices in my head.[2]

You have full permission to write a terrible first draft. Really. We're so conditioned to think of correcting and editing as a sign of weakness that it can be a huge barrier to overcome. When I ghostwrite books for my clients I never send them the very first draft. Heaven forbid! The points are in the wrong order, the writing is clumsy, and there aren't nearly enough stories and analogies to pep it up.

---

[2] Anne Lamott, *Bird by Bird*, Anchor, 1994.

Figuratively speaking, the creative part of your brain is separate from the rational, editing part; if you try to make the two work together you'll become exhausted and demotivated pretty quickly. Instead, enjoy the freedom of letting your words flow without criticism when you begin; later you can go back and put them in order.

Give yourself a break

Have you ever had a brilliant idea when you were least expecting it? I have. It's because our minds need to be uncluttered for our creativity to burst through. When I'm deep into my writing and juggling three or four thoughts at once, I'm completely convinced that I can't move away from my desk for a moment or I'll forget what I'm doing.

Then the doorbell goes and cursing, I answer it. But lo and behold, that complex problem of how I was going to combine idea A with thought C, via paragraph B, is magically solved by the addition of one simple sentence. Every time, I wonder why I didn't give myself a break when writing seemed like it was getting complicated. One day maybe I'll learn.

Don't write the book yourself

There's an alternative to you spending time at your keyboard writing, and that's to work with a ghostwriter. This is more common than you might think; it's estimated that 50% of nonfiction bestsellers are ghostwritten, and when a major celebrity or politician is involved the figure rises even higher. This makes sense. When someone's capable of earning good money doing what they're brilliant at, they're not likely to put their life on hold for several months to write a book. Nor do they want to go through the learning curve of developing their writing skills and honing their craft. No, they let a ghostwriter take care of that.

You might wonder what this has to do with you, but surely you want to become a celebrity too? Not necessarily a global superstar, but a business celebrity – the go-to person for what you do; the expert who's asked to speak at events (and is paid for it); the coach who has clients lining up to pay premium prices; and the author who's quoted in other people's books and blogs. It's worth looking at how a ghostwriter can benefit you.

- *You'll save a lot of time.* This is how a ghostwriter saves you money. If you factor in the months of planning, drafting, and editing a book, what else could you be doing with that time and energy? Helping more people, working with more clients, and developing the back-end of your business to benefit from a book? These activities earn you income, which your business book will eventually boost to a new level. I estimate I save my clients an average of 137 hours per book by ghostwriting it for them,[3] and that takes into account the time they put into the process as well.

- *Your book will be readable.* You may be gifted or experienced at writing, enjoy it, and be happy to

---

[3] See my blog 'How Much Time Do You Save Working with a Ghostwriter?' for a breakdown: www.marketingtwentyone.co.uk/time-save-ghostwriter/

make time for it; if so, you should definitely write your own book. But if this isn't you, you can hand the task to a professional just as you outsource your logo design to a graphic designer and your accounts to an accountant. I don't mind telling you, I never touch my own tax return; I'd rather sleep at night than be worrying about whether I've made a monumental mistake with the figures, and I know my accountant will make sure it's done correctly.

- *You'll gain a fresh, objective view of your topic.* A ghostwriter can pull out ideas and concepts from your mind that you didn't even know were there. They'll then write about them in a way that wins over your readers, taking your book from pedestrian to professional. As ghostwriter Andrew Crofts explains in his book *Ghostwriting*, 'A ghost can be an enormous help in turning an expert into a great teacher, in being the one who translates the knowledge that is in the expert's head into a language that others with none of that knowledge can understand.'[4]

- *Your book will happen.* When there's no imperative to finish a book, the manuscript draft has a habit of staying unfinished, or worse, in its creator's head. And if you're the kind of person who loves starting things but gets bored half way through implementing them, handing the writing task to someone whose livelihood depends on completing it is a smart move.

---

[4] Andrew Crofts, *Ghostwriting*, A&C Black, 2004.

- *A publishing deal will come more easily.* Publishers love professional ghostwriters because they know the book will be completed on time and be a clear and persuasive read. So if you're seeking a traditional publisher, it's worth letting them know if you're working with a quality ghostwriter who's creating the manuscript in your voice.

How does ghostwriting work?

A quality ghostwriter sees themselves as a strategist as well as a writer. They'll spend time understanding what you want to achieve with your book, who it's for, whether there's an angle on it that would help it sell more easily, and how it will boost your business. They'll also work with you to create an outline, and interview you to understand what's in your head. Turning your thoughts into writing on the page, they'll take care to write in your voice so the book reads as if it comes from your hand and not theirs – this is a consummate skill. If you've already written a whole or partly completed manuscript they can also re-write it for you, producing a polished final article.

However, there are some factors to consider when working with a ghostwriter. You need to be prepared to delegate your most cherished thoughts and opinions to someone else, and be able to trust them to craft them in your voice; this means selecting your writer with care. Speak to as many as you need in order to find the right one for you. Sensing if you have a connection with them, and checking that they have experience in writing the genre of book you're after, is more important than if they have knowledge about your topic. An experienced ghostwriter will be happy to spend time talking with you and showing you examples of their work, and will be sussing you out as much as you are them; they know from experience how essential the right chemistry is. Also, be prepared to wait for the right one to become available because the best ghostwriters are sometimes in high demand.

How much can you expect to pay for a ghostwriter? The answer is the same as, 'What can you expect to pay for a car?' It depends on your expectations and the results you're after. You can hire a low-cost writer from one of the mass market freelancer sites for between a few hundred pounds and £3,000. Some are native English speakers but many are not, which means they don't have the nuanced language skills to make your book shine. I've seen the output of some of these writers and it's clear they've harvested much of their content from the Internet. Their writing isn't distinctive and wouldn't make you look good.

Professional book ghostwriters, on the other hand, are a different breed. They see their job as being to write your book with fluency, skill, and interest. They'll focus on gaining and keeping your readers' attention, leading them through your arguments with persuasion and clarity, and will deliver on time. They can also have connections in the publishing industry and may be able to advise you on other aspects of your book such as self-publishing, marketing, and promotion. For this kind of ghostwriter, expect to pay from £25,000 and even into six figures. If that seems like a lot, think how much more it will cost you if you don't get your book out there at all because you're not confident about your writing or can't move past your first draft. It's your reputation on the line; it's your name on the cover; and it's your book. Make it a transformational one.

How does coaching work?

If a ghostwriter isn't in your budget, or if writing your book yourself means a lot to you, it can still feel daunting to branch out alone. One way of dealing with this is to work with a book coach. A coach is someone who's written plenty of books of their own, and who's managed to unpick the process so they can help you to do the same. It's important to choose one who specialises in your type of book; for instance, a coach working with fiction writers wouldn't be for you if you're creating a how-to guide.

A business book coach will help you decide what kind of book to write for your business (and understand the world of business too), create your outline with you, give you sound tips and advice on planning and writing, and hold your hand all the way through. They'll also work with you to create a marketing plan and advise you on the different publishing routes, using their contacts to give you the best recommendations for professionals to help you complete your work. In my experience of coaching many clients through to publishing their books, the benefits they receive from the process are twofold: their motivation is kept high through the regular contact with their coach, and they end up with a more professional and well-written book than if they'd gone it alone.

There's a cost to coaching. But think about it for a moment: what would it cost you *not* to put your book out there? Your aim is to make a return on your investment many times over once your book is published, so if you need help it makes sense to ask for it.

Now you know how to write your book, it's time to consider the editing process. This is what we'll look at next.

What we've covered

- ❖ Most of the hurdles to keeping writing are in your head – this means you have various ways of getting around them.

- ❖ Speaking your book is a powerful way of avoiding writer's block, as is not caring about perfection at first.

- ❖ A ghostwriter can turn the thoughts in your head into a polished and engaging book, with minimal time and effort from yourself.

- ❖ A book coach can smooth the way to both starting and finishing your book.

Chapter 11

Editing your book

The five-step process for making it simple

Writing is easy. All you have to do is cross out the wrong words.
Mark Twain

When I had a haircut recently I asked the hairdresser what could be done to make my fine hair look thicker, and she advised slicing some layers into it. I was surprised – surely that would mean less hair, not more? But she was right. Chopping out hair in strategic places added volume and structure, making what was left look far more enticing (or so I like to think). This is the way it is with your writing. What you take out leaves space for the important stuff to come through, giving your book interest and shape. Don't be afraid to drop some of your writing on the cutting room floor. This, folks, is what we call editing.

Why is editing so important? Think of watching a fight scene in a movie. You're engrossed in the action, wincing at each body blow and flinching as a nasty one causes blood to pour from the hero's head. Will he make it through so he can save the day? Will he even survive? You forget you're in a cinema – it's just 'real' to you. Then, as you peek from behind your fingers to see if he'll manage to prise himself from the grip of his evil enemy, you notice something incongruous on the left side of the screen. It's the edge of the scenery, which only shows for a second but long enough to distract you from the action. This glitch reminds you that you're only watching a movie after all. For that moment you lose your sense of flow – not for long, but enough to spoil your fun.

Now imagine you're reading a book, and have the same experience from being unable to work out what the author is trying to say. Or maybe there's a clumsily constructed sentence or misspelled word. It's the same jarring experience, but with one important difference. You're unlikely to walk out of a cinema if you stumble over a split second in a film, but with a book it's all too easy to put it down, intend to pick it up again later, and never get around to it because your last encounter wasn't terribly positive. This is why editing is as much a part of creating a brilliant business book as planning and writing it are.

When to start editing your book

It's a glorious moment when your first draft is complete, or it will be if you get that far. Many authors don't – they polish their first couple of chapters until they can see their faces in them, start to contemplate the remaining 40,000 words, and then… it feels overwhelming, so they put the book 'on hold'. This the main reason I suggest (nay, insist) you stop yourself doing any serious editing until you've finished the first draft of your whole book.

There are other benefits to this too:

- you can't polish what you've written until you have the whole book in front of you – the flow won't be obvious until then, and

- if you edit as you go along you delay the completion of your first draft, which denies you the satisfaction of seeing the whole work that you – yes *you* – wrote.

So 'draft hot, edit cold', as they say. I'm about to show you how to transform your imperfect first draft into a thing of beauty.

How to edit your book

Editing is a simple process but it can feel like a big deal, so here's a systematic way to do it. Believe me, when you're wrestling thousands of words into shape a procedure comes in handy. Also, revising your draft is a 'left brain' activity which entails being objective about what you've written, so following a set of guidelines feeds nicely into that mindset.

Step 1: be ready

Wait at least a week or two between finishing your first draft and editing it. We read faster than we write, so you won't have a sense of the pace of the finished book as experienced by your readers until you've allowed some time to pass. Also, you need space to forget the writing of it: the highs, the lows, the terrible sentences that didn't work but which you decided to leave in because (quite rightly) you wanted to press on. And you want to experience the pleasant surprises, too. It's like when you come home from being away and see your house anew; it's not just that damp patch on the wall that screams at you, but the bright beauty of the colourful rug you'd stopped appreciating.

Next print out your manuscript, numbering your pages and ensuring each chapter starts on a new page. Yes, you'll hear the trees crying, but it's the only way. We skim read on screen but we read more slowly from the printed page, so if you rely on a digital version you'll miss countless errors. The bonus of this is that you'll feel mightily impressed by the vast amount of words you've generated – it's starting to look like a real book.

Now it becomes fun. Grab a pad of sticky notes, a pen, and some blank sheets of A4 paper. Turn one of your sheets horizontally and put the names of each chapter across the top (you may need more than one sheet). You'll be sticking your notes in columns below. Find yourself a cosy spot where you can read your manuscript away from your normal writing desk – a fresh perspective helps. Go outside if it's sunny, but don't forget to weigh down your pages or you'll have the same experience as I did in my garden while editing a client's manuscript (frogs all over the neighbourhood are still reading it to this day).

Step 2: be mentally prepared

Return to your original book strategy and outline document. Read it through again. If anything has changed in the meantime make a note, but otherwise remind yourself why you're writing this book, who it's for, and what the 'gold' within it is. You should be thinking: 'What's the point of this book? Who would read it? And why?' Write your answers in bold at the top of a blank sheet of paper and keep it visible at all times while you're editing.

Moving forward, I suggest you set aside several hours each for steps three, four, and five and do them in no more than one or two sessions per step. This allows you to hold your whole book in your head – helpful for spotting gaps and repetitions.

Step 3: edit for content and readability

In this step you're not worrying about style, only content. If you see the odd stylistic mistake by all means correct it if it's simple, but try not to become distracted. Take one chapter at a time and before you start reading it, note down the following questions at the top of each chapter (one sentence only per answer):

- What's the purpose of this chapter?
- How does it fit into the purpose of this book?
- If my readers could take away only one point from the chapter, what would it be?

- What impression do I want them to have by the end?

Now read through, taking note of the following:

- Does anything in the chapter not serve the purpose you identified above? If not, cross it out or make a note to move it somewhere more useful by jotting a remark on a sticky note and placing it on your chapter heading sheet. It doesn't matter how beautifully the section is written, or how much you love it, it needs to go.

- Are your points ordered in a logical way so they make sense for your reader? If not, draw some arrows to re-order them.

- If you were in your readers' shoes, would you need more information about a particular topic? Don't assume they know everything you do.

- Have you referred to anything coming later or earlier in the book? If so, don't try and find it now but jot it on a sticky note and place it under that chapter heading on your sheet. You'll use it to check for consistency later.

- If it occurs to you that new material needs to be added, write it on one of your blank sheets and insert it into the relevant place in your manuscript.

- Have you repeated stories or points from other chapters? If you think you might have done, note these on your sticky notes and check later.

- Do you need to do more research on an area? Could you create or insert an invitation to download a lead magnet in certain places? If so, this goes on a sticky note too.

Step four: make your changes

Return to your computer and make the necessary changes, saving the chapters as a second draft. You can bin the sticky notes as you go along (a satisfying process, I find) and keep the ones that need more work. While you're re-writing, stay alert for any further changes you might need to make but avoid making stylistic ones; you're focusing on top-line flow here, not elegance of language. Cutting and pasting is usually fine, along with a basic effort to make the joins look pretty; think patchwork rather than fine needlework.

Step five: edit for style

Print out the whole manuscript once more (again, ignore the weeping trees). This time read it aloud so you gain a feel for the sound and rhythm of your writing, because when a word or phrase snags for you it'll snag for your reader too. Scribble a correction on your manuscript and read it again. Reading aloud is something most authors don't do, and which will instantly put you ahead of the pack – when you try it, you'll see why it makes such a difference.

If you find your mind wandering, your readers' minds will wander as well. Does your writing need more interest, more punch? Is it too long-winded? Could it do with a story, an interesting fact, or a touch of controversy to liven it up? Are you making use of metaphors, images, and interesting words to avoid a dry reading experience? Trust your instincts here. Also, ensure your chapters make consistent use of headings and sub-headings.

Pay attention to the rhythm of your sentences. Cut any jargon, woolly phrases or words that don't add to your meaning, and re-work awkward sentences by saying aloud what you mean and working from there. The most common impact of this process is the removal of the crutch words I talked about earlier – these cloud the message you're imparting.

After you've done this, return to your computer and input your changes. Give yourself a week or two's break and then re-read the entire manuscript one more time (on screen this time if you prefer), tweaking as you go along.

You're done! Feel free to reward yourself in whatever excessively indulgent way you like. You've earned it.

Do you need a professional editor?

'Can't I just ask someone else to edit my manuscript?' is a question I'm often asked. My answer is: 'You must!' There's no substitute for an objective, professional editor assessing and developing your manuscript – it's definitely not a step or investment you should skip. It's easy to spot an author-editing job – you can tell from the confused trains of thought, repeated words, awkward sentences, and sloppy grammar. Don't let this be your book.

However, it's hugely valuable if you can go through the process above before you hand over your book to a professional editor. For a start you'll save money, because editors are a canny lot and – understandably – tend to charge more for writing that's heavy work. But also because you're more likely to end up with a result you're happy with; the more you've revised your manuscript to your satisfaction, the more of 'you' there will be in it.

There are three basic kinds of editor: a structural or developmental editor, a copy editor, and a proof reader. A structural editor covers off step 3 of the editing process (content and flow) and a copy editor step 5 (style, grammar, and spelling). You can see it makes sense to have your book structurally edited before you have it copy edited, allowing you to make top-level changes before you finesse the language and correct the details. A proof reader is an absolute must, but only at the very end of the process once your book is formatted for print. They'll dot every 'i' and cross every 't' to perfection, in a way that only someone who's never read your book can do; they have a 'cold eye' and don't read your book to appreciate the tone and ideas, but to ruthlessly weed out errors. After your manuscript has been proof read, *don't make any more changes* no matter how much you're desperate to. It's a recipe for glitches to creep in.

I give suggestions about how to find an editor in Chapter 13.

Beta readers

To be objective about one's own book is pretty much impossible, so this is where a trusty team of beta readers comes in. Beta readers are an author's secret weapon

– they're sample people in your target readership who will give you honest feedback before you come to the final edit. Everyone has beta readers available to them, they just don't always know it. Try mining these for yours:

- past and current clients;
- experts in your field;
- people on your email list; and
- trusted colleagues and connections.

Remember, you don't want feedback from any old person, but from the kind of reader who would buy your book *in real life*. This probably excludes your best friend, your partner, and your mum. It can be distracting and even damaging to hear from these people that they 'don't understand the second chapter', when to someone in your target audience it would make complete sense. A more likely scenario is that they say they love it all, which gives you a warm glow but isn't the feedback you need.

When you have a small team of up to half a dozen beta readers together, send them your draft manuscript when it's in a finalised enough state for you to bear anyone else's eyes to be on it. Ask them to be objective and not to hold back from suggesting changes; you can use the track changes function in Word, or put it up as a Google Doc and turn comments on. Here are some suggestions as to what you can ask them to do:

- point out any areas they feel confused by;
- comment on the areas that most interest or enlighten them; and

- say when they feel bored.

Most of all, you want to find out what they see as the main point of your book. Have they changed their views or learned anything new? You may be surprised to discover it wasn't what you had in mind.

When you're done, you're done

Thankfully we authors aren't brain surgeons. We don't have to get things right first time, and we also have the luxury of making as many changes as we like for as long as we feel the need. To use another medical analogy, the act of writing a book has often been compared to pregnancy and birth. However, although it certainly takes months (along with some blood, sweat, and tears – resulting in a beautiful newborn), this is where the similarity ends. A baby has a self-imposed deadline and will appear at some point whether you're ready or not; a book has no such built-in timer and if you're not careful it can carry on gestating forever.

Show me an author who couldn't go through every book they've published and pinpoint, page by page, what's wrong with it and I'll show you... well, someone who doesn't exist. You need to have some way of drawing a line under your quest for perfection. Try to move away from your intellectual mind and listen to your instincts here. How do you decide to finish anything? You just somehow know when enough is enough. It's the same sixth sense that tells a film director when to make the final edit, or a painter when to put down their brushes.

But if you want a concrete answer to when to stop editing and press the publish button, here it is – it's not perfect but it's the best I've got. I've even created a checklist for you.

- ☐ Your book is the right length for your goal
- ☐ It makes sense
- ☐ It's interesting; in other words, it contains plenty of stories, anecdotes, analogies, and examples
- ☐ When you read it aloud your voice naturally rises and falls in line with the variety of tone and pace, showing it has rhythm
- ☐ It's backed up by enough facts and research for your readers' needs
- ☐ Ways of marketing your business are embedded in it

You're now done with creating your manuscript, and it's almost about to turn into a book! But before we dive into publishing, let's look at a few final elements to put in place before you're ready to press 'send'.

What we've covered

- Finish your first draft before you start editing.
- Use a systematic editing process to ensure your book is clear, persuasive, and that there are minimal spelling or grammar errors.
- Ask beta readers to review your manuscript before you finalise it – they're your real-world audience.

Chapter 12

The last hard yard

Finish your book!

I went for years not finishing anything. Because, of course, when you finish something you can be judged.
Erica Jong, bestselling author

So near and yet so far. Your manuscript is in your hot little hands and it's looking pretty darn good. Congratulations – you've achieved what few others have done, which is to finish writing your book. But there are a few more areas to consider before you can publish it. You're almost there, you're just dotting the i's and crossing the t's.

Permissions

Here's where you consider the legalities of what you've written. Is it okay to use other people's ideas and words in your book? This is normal. After all, none of us comes up with consistently original material – we 'stand on the shoulders of giants' in our work, learning from those who've paved the way before us. It's likely you're also doing the same for others too, even if you don't realise it yet. But consider this: You wouldn't want the authors of the future to swipe your material without attributing it to you, would you? Aside from the ethical issues there are legal implications to doing this, so let's take a look at where you stand when you want to pick other experts' brains.

Of course, I'm not a lawyer and this is not to be taken as legal advice. If you have any doubts, speak to your editor (if you have a publisher) or consult a legal boffin.

Using someone else's ideas

The good news is you can't copyright an idea or concept, so you're free to use ones generated by other people in your book. It's good manners to credit them, though. Mention who you gained your idea from and even the book you read it in if that's the case; this also presents you as well informed and up to date.

Using someone else's words

The less good news is you can copyright words. When someone writes something and publishes it, whether it be in a book, their blog, a letter, or any other platform, they automatically own the copyright to it. That means you can't take their words and replicate them in your book without their permission. It doesn't matter whether you credit them or not, the words are theirs.

If you quote a large amount of text for the purpose of critiquing or reviewing it, this affects you. You also need permission to use it for other purposes, such as taking a chunk of a poem to round off your book or to start a chapter. Extracts from newspapers or magazines are a no-no, as is lifting illustrations, designs, and diagrams you've found elsewhere. Song lyrics are a definite one to stay away from as they're owned by the music label (or whoever owns the copyright) and are notoriously hard to get permission for.

This sounds onerous, but it's not actually as restricting as it might seem because there are a number of work-arounds. I've listed them here, but again I'm not a lawyer so if you're in any doubt you need to seek expert advice.

- In Europe, copyright only lasts for the author's lifetime and for 70 years after the end of the year in which they died. So if you're quoting from material dating from a long time ago, you're *probably* fine.

- There's a get-out clause called 'fair dealing' which allows you to quote other people's words under certain circumstances. Fair dealing isn't a law in itself and therefore isn't watertight, but it provides guidance for the publishing profession. The elements of fair dealing you'll be interested in are:

  - if your quote is no more than around 300 words, it's fair dealing as long as you credit the author with their name, the title of the publication, the page number if relevant, the publisher, and when it was published. You can do this in a footnote like this: author name, *X Book Title*, page x, publisher name, year of publication.

- ○ in principle you can also quote up to half a page of play text or up to a total of 40 lines from a poem, as long as it's not more than a quarter of the whole.

- An exception to the fair dealing rule is when the quoted text sums up the meaning of the whole work, and thereby isn't equivalent to a small element of it.

- Song titles are fine to quote as they're considered to be in the public domain, even if the lyrics aren't.

If you want to use someone else's copyrighted material and it doesn't fall into the exclusions above, you need to ask permission from whoever owns the copyright. That's usually the publisher. They may not reply (because it's a hassle for them) or if they do they may charge a fee which can range from affordable to eye-watering. How much trouble you take will depend on the strength of your feeling about including the material, which may by now be sorely tested.

Front and back matter

It's hard to say those words without sounding a little rude, but humour aside, these are separate sections of your book that you may want to include in addition to your main chapters. None of them is compulsory but I'll describe them here so you know how to create your own.

Praise

If you have lots of reviews and testimonials for your book, you can create a section for them at the beginning. They're highly persuasive for potential buyers, and you can start collecting them as soon as you have a rough version of your manuscript ready to show people. If you write a second edition of your book you can include post-publication reviews too. Pick no more than half a dozen of your juiciest and most tempting critiques – you're using them to wow your readers.

Foreword

This comes before your first chapter and is written by someone who admires your work. It sets the scene for your book, bigging it up for your readers before they dive in. Think of it as a more in-depth and thoughtful version of the introduction a compere gives to the next comedian to come on stage: 'He was one of the first acts to dominate the northern circuit with his breakthrough performance "Shakespeare in Mime". He's mentored countless new comedians, all of whom are now funnier than him. And he's come all the way from the job centre especially for tonight's performance. Put your hands together for… Johnny Comedy!!!!!'

I exaggerate, of course. But this does reflect what a good foreword does: it primes your reader to be enthusiastic about the book they're set to read. It should therefore be written by a known name or authority in your field – someone your readers have heard of and would trust. It can also make reference to why they're qualified to recommend your book, and highlight the benefits of reading it.

Something to watch out for: valuable though these sections can be, they delay the reading of your book and can frustrate your readers if they're too long. They also take up prime real estate in the Amazon 'Look Inside' feature, so readers can't check out as much of your content as they might want to. It's a balancing act. Just like Praise, it's not compulsory to have a Foreword and many books do without one, so if you're struggling with who to ask, don't worry about it.

Acknowledgements

This is your chance to make the people who've helped you with your book feel special. Think publisher, ghostwriter, editor, foreword writer, beta readers, book coach, colleagues, and anyone else who's had direct input. Again it's not compulsory, but there's nothing like having written a whole damn book to make you empathise with the Oscar winner who gushes their thanks to everyone from their agent to their mother 'who gave birth to me'. This section is usually found at the end of the book.

'About the author' page

This is the one area that is vital for a business author. It tells your readers who you are, why you have the credibility to write this book, and how they can work with you further. It usually goes straight after your last chapter, and is the one place you have complete permission to promote yourself openly without looking like a salesperson. So make the most of it.

It sounds like a contradiction but this page isn't about you, it's about your readers. What do they want to know about you which would be interesting and helpful to them? It's probably not a dry list of qualifications but a summary of what you've done in your work that's led you to this point, the elements of it that inspire you, and where you focus your professional energies. You can also include testimonials, other books you've written, major talks you've given, or work of yours in the media. Make sure you add a reference to how people can find out more about you; this could be your website, social media, or even an email address if you feel comfortable giving it out.

Write your 'About the author' page in the third person (so it's 'he' or 'she', not 'I'), and in a warm and friendly tone. Try and make it a bit interesting and fun; it should encourage your readers to want to find out more about you. This isn't the place to hold back on your credentials - don't get all modest on me here!

Now you're finally ready for that moment every author dreams of: the day they can send off their manuscript to the publisher. A bit like when a parent waves off their newly fledged offspring after they've graduated from college, this may feel like 'goodbye' for your book. But don't worry — just like that parent, you'll see it back plenty of times before it's fully flown.

What we've covered

❖ Make sure you're legally allowed to quote material from other authors' works before you include them in your book.

❖ Do you want a page for testimonials and also a foreword? Now's the time to start thinking about them.

❖ Your 'About the Author' page is a vital element of your business book.

Chapter 13

Publishing your book

The publishing options

> *Writers live twice.*
> Natalie Goldberg, bestselling author

If you visit the Treasures room at the British Library in London, you'll see the original publishing contract for John Milton's epic Renaissance poem *Paradise Lost*. It reveals he was to be paid £5 on signing, £5 after 1,300 copies had been sold, and £10 after a further 1,300 (sadly he died before this last become a reality). A cynical mind might come to the conclusion that the traditional publishing industry has changed little since the seventeenth century – certainly in terms of advances and royalty rates!

Today, however, publishing your book can be as easy and as profitable as you make it, whatever route you take. I'm lucky enough to know, and regularly speak with, many publishers of all descriptions, so although I'm not a publisher myself I understand the sector from an author's perspective. And here is what I've learned.

The easy way to pick your publishing route

As a business author today, you live in lucky times. Until a few years ago there were only two ways to publish your book: go for a traditional publishing deal or resort to a 'vanity' publisher and pay them to put your book out there. Nowadays you have a richer choice, and I like to see deciding how to publish your business book as a bit like choosing between red and white wine – you do it by considering the occasion and your personal taste. It's not as if red is better than white, or vice versa, it's just a question of your circumstances and preferences.

The wine list (or, less excitingly, publishing options)
So what are these publishing choices? They fall into three camps.

- *Traditional publisher* – such as Penguin Random House, Hachette, HarperCollins, Pan Macmillan, Bloomsbury, Simon & Schuster, and Wiley – although there are also many smaller, independent publishing houses. These guys take care of everything for you so you can get on with your business (or writing your next book). That sounds brilliant, but there are some drawbacks as you'll see below.

- *Self-publishing* – this is the DIY option, in which you outsource the various elements of publishing your book such as typesetting, cover design, and printing, to your own suppliers. You then project manage the process of publishing your book yourself.

- *Hybrid or partner publisher* – a company that publishes your book in exchange for a fee, thereby freeing you from the tasks you'd undertake as a self-publisher. The best ones are run by publishing experts who can also give you quality advice on how to position and promote your book in its marketplace. A helpful way to look at the difference between a partner and a traditional publisher is to compare the relationship you have to each of them: to a traditional publisher you're a supplier (of the manuscript), whereas to the partner publisher you're a client.

Your next task is to peruse this list of pros and cons.

Traditional publishing

The pros

- *Prestige*: there's an unwritten assumption that if you've landed a traditional deal, your book must be high quality. And there's some truth in that assumption, because traditional publishers have high standards and accept only a fraction of the manuscripts they receive.

- *Validation*: it's natural to have doubts about your book, so it being acquired by an agent or publisher can be a confidence booster.

- *Free services*: the publisher takes care of the cover design, typesetting, print, and all other tasks and costs associated with putting your book into the world.

- *Width of distribution*: you're more likely to have your book sold in bricks-and-mortar bookstores than the other publishing routes, although it's still unlikely (the stores only display a fraction of books published each year).

- *Editing*: the opportunity to build a fruitful working relationship with a professional editor.

- *Some marketing*: they help with this, although most of your book marketing will be down to you.

The cons

- *Time*: publishers and agents reject the vast majority of book proposals, and it can take several months (if ever) to hear back from them. After that, waiting up to a year for your book to appear isn't unusual.

- *The changing nature of readers' perceptions*: it's no longer the case that readers judge a book according to what company published it. Think of your favourite nonfiction book right now. Can you tell me who the publisher is? I thought not.

- *Copyright*: you have to license this to your publisher so may not be able to have your book translated, recorded onto audio, re-edited, and so on.

- *Ownership*: your book isn't 'yours' anymore. Want to decide on your title and cover design? You can give an opinion but it's not your decision. You'll also have to make changes to your manuscript to match the publisher's requirements.

- *Royalties*: a wide range, but way lower than the other publishing options (and advances are rare). Also, some publishers expect you to buy a number of your own books for you to sell yourself; this can cost several thousand pounds.

- *Freedom to market, leverage and sell your book yourself*: they may not allow you to do what you like to promote and sell your book (such as sell your own copies at conferences), although they'll certainly expect you to do most of the marketing legwork.

Self-publishing

The pros

- *Full control*: it's your book, your way. This is attractive if you have an entrepreneurial mindset.

- *Royalties*: you don't pay publishers' royalties, and therefore keep all your sales revenue.

- *Timing and flexibility*: you can decide when you want your book to appear, and it can be quick.

- *Leverage*: once your book is out there you can use it to promote your business however you like.

- *Audience*: if your book is intended for a small market, self-publishing may be the only option for you.

The cons

- *Less prestige*: you won't have a known publisher's name on the cover.

- *Up-front costs*: you have to pay your suppliers before you make any money from sales, although new, high-quality print-on-demand services reduce the up-front investment.

- *Time and energy*: you're project managing a process that requires a steep learning curve – this takes up your time and energy and is probably only worthwhile if you're planning on writing more than one book (and even then…).

- *Quality*: it's up to you to make sure your book looks professional, and you're not a publishing expert.

- *Distribution*: you don't have an 'in' into the major distributors, so you're limited to selling online and via your own channels.

- *Lack of marketing support*: you're on your own unless you pay someone to help you.

Hybrid or partner publishing

The pros

- *Expertise*: a top-notch partner publisher will advise you on your options based on what you want to achieve with your book, and they know the industry and its suppliers well. They also understand what metadata to include in your ISBN in order to maximise your book's discoverability.

- *Control*: you decide how you want your book to look and what to do with it once it's published.

- *Time*: you don't have to spend your precious time co-ordinating different suppliers, and partner publishers work more quickly than traditional ones.

- *Distribution*: some can get your book into the major book distributors.

- *Leverage*: once your book is out there, you can use it to promote your business however you like.

- *Royalties*: you keep a higher percentage than with a traditional publisher.

The cons

- *Cost*: you're paying for the publisher's time, materials, and expertise, so it will cost you more than self- or traditional publishing. You'll also need to pay them up front, before you make any money from your book.

- *Loss of some royalties and copyright compared to self-publishing:* depending on the publisher, they may take some of your royalties and/or your copyright for a set period of time. This isn't the case with all, so check.

- *Marketing support:* this is often an extra cost, so while they may advise you on marketing, you'll need to pay for it if you want hands-on support (although this is often the case with a traditional publisher too).

- *Choice overload:* there are many companies to choose from, with some being excellent and others to avoid. Do your research carefully, talking to the owner about what you want your book to do for you. Any reputable firm will be happy to give you their time and opinion as a starting point.

Which option will you choose?

It depends on what you want your book to achieve, how quickly you want to get it out there, and how much control over it you want to maintain.

This is best understood though examples. Say you're a speaker hoping to sell copies of your book at your talks, which means a print book will be important to you. You won't be selling a high proportion of them through retailers and you want them to be ready as quickly as possible in order to maximise sales at your next conference keynote. Partner or self-publishing is probably best for you. But what if you're an online business owner, wanting to use your book to drive traffic to your website and encourage readers to sign up to your list? You may find a short e-book is what you need, and you can self-publish that without much difficulty. On the other hand if you're a well-respected thought-leader wanting a book to build your authority, and aren't worried about it taking a long time, a traditionally published book – with the prestige it brings – might fit you best. The same applies if your book is on a mainstream popular topic and is written in an accessible style.

In other words, think about what your business needs before you decide which route to take.

Traditional publishing: what you need to know

Going for the traditional publishing option can be seductive because of the kudos and lack of financial outlay involved, and it's certainly a good option if it matches your goals and you're willing to devote the effort to attracting a deal. However, when I work with authors favouring this route, I find myself talking to them in the same way I would if one of my friends were to announce they wanted to become a movie star: 'That sounds great – but you might want to think of a fall-back plan in case it doesn't work out.' Ask yourself, is the prestige and validation of being traditionally published going to make a difference to what you get out of your book, or is it only the nice feeling that you're chasing? You have to really want this, because it's not an easy route.

However, if you won't be dissuaded, consider the characteristics such a publisher looks for.

- *A book that's commercially viable.* To a traditional publisher your book is a product they will manufacture and sell, so they want one they can shift in large enough numbers to make the financial risk worthwhile.

- *A book that's aimed at the right audience for them.* Some publishers specialise in mass market books, others in niche titles. Even the latter will want to be sure they can sell thousands of copies, though.

- *A book written by an author with a strong marketing platform.* A traditional publisher will look first to see how large your personal audience is before they'll consider signing you up. Do you already have an email list and social media following consisting of multiple thousands? Do you regularly speak at large events? Are you willing to spend your own time and money on promoting your book to the right people, and at volume? The marketing of your book will be largely your job, and although your publisher might support you they prefer to go with authors who are a sure bet.

You'll also need to write a book proposal in order to attract the attention of an agent or publisher (an agent is someone who collects proposals and submits to publishers the ones he or she thinks they'd be interested in, in exchange for a commission). This is a significant undertaking but extremely worthwhile to do at the beginning of any book journey – if for no other reason than that it helps you to be clear about all aspects of your book.

So how do you write a book proposal? Some publishers ask you to use their own proposal format but others leave it up to you. If you're creating your own, here's a brief outline of what to produce – you can see it's worth spending a fair few hours on it. To make it look professional, create a cover page with your proposed title and subtitle, your name and contact details, and maybe a picture of you. Then add a table of contents. Here's what goes inside:

Your proposed title and subtitle
What you suggest the book be called (the publisher will have the final say).

Book specifications
Include:

- The approximate number of words;
- The format, e.g. paperback, e-book;
- Illustrations – how many and what kind (approximately).

Summary
This is the core marketing rationale for your book and should take a couple of paragraphs. It answers these questions: What's your book about? What's the point of it? Who's it for? What will your readers gain from it? What makes you the best person to write it, and why now? If this doesn't strike the agent or publisher as interesting and relevant, they'll read no further.

Your thesis

Depending on the nature of your topic, you may find it helpful to write a short number of paragraphs explaining the central concept of your book.

Key features

The three to four key features of your book as bullet points. Make them reader-related, as they'll be used by your publisher for distributor sales copy.

Target audience

Who's your book for? If you've done your book planning this will be a cinch. But you'll also want to consider the size of your market because that's what a publisher will care about; use the Office for National Statistics website and other sources to quantify it. Also, are there any secondary audiences you can think of such as academics, students, or people in related fields?

Author bio

This is best written in the third person. You're answering these questions: Why you? And what's your marketing platform? What qualifies you to write this book? What media do you appear in regularly? What's the size of your audience? If you've written any other books before, give sales figures. Remember, the publisher is concerned with how many copies it can sell so it wants to know your credentials, both business and social.

Competing titles

Go through the five or ten successful and well-known books your proposed readers could choose to buy instead of yours, and summarise them in a list. Explain why yours is different from each, but without being critical – you're seeking to prove there's an established market for your book but at the same time why there's a gap in it for your own. For instance the other titles could be out of date, written for an alternative audience, have dissimilarities to yours in the way the topic is approached, or be written in a different style.

Marketing and promotion

This is the nub of your proposal. How do you plan to promote your book so that it sells thousands of copies? Think about what media outlets your target readers pay attention to and which you could appear in. Can you count on any endorsements from big names in your field, or invitations to speak at large events? What's your email list and social media size? Are there any other promotional opportunities you could exploit, such as workshops, tours, your website, or your blog? Quantify the size of your platforms.

If you're not able to convince a publisher that you have the marketing clout to promote your book effectively, they'll justifiably wonder why they would take a punt on investing in it. So approach this with confidence and show you know it's your responsibility to do this bit well.

Table of contents

If you've done your book planning this is easy. Write a list of chapters with a summary of each. The aim is to give the publisher a clear idea of what the content of your book will consist of, and a flavour of how it will be written. Some of this may change once you start writing the book, and that's fine.

Sample chapters

Include one or two chapters; not the introduction, but ones that showcase the tone and content of the book. The publisher will want to see what experience a reader will have of it, but in sample form.

If you're still up for going for a traditional publisher, your next move is to buy yourself a copy of *Writers' and Artists' Yearbook* which lists them all, along with agents. Or if you have any form of personal connection to a publishing house, use it. Then send your proposal, along with a compelling covering email, to the publishers you think will be most suited to your book and keep your fingers crossed. Persistence is the name of the game, so if you don't hear back from someone or are turned down, keep going. JK Rowling was famously rejected by 12 publishers for *Harry Potter* before she ended up with Bloomsbury, so you never know!

Self-publishing: what you need to know

Self-publishing your book deserves a guide in its own right (and they exist – see the 'Further resources' section for recommendations), so this is a brief overview of the areas you'll need to cover. The main thing to bear in mind is that without a professional publishing team you'll need to be your own quality controller. Publishers don't necessarily have access to better suppliers than you, it's their high standards that set them apart from the hasty amateur.

Editing

As a minimum you'll need a copy editor and a proof reader, and possibly a structural editor too. Please don't skip these steps, even if they may be the most costly and time consuming elements of the process. To find an editor, ask for recommendations or check out the acknowledgements sections of books you've enjoyed – editors are often thanked for their contribution and you can contact them direct. Alternatively, specialist online freelancer sites such as Reedsy and the Society for Editors and Proofreaders are helpful ports of call.

Cover design

When you think about how you search for books and decide which ones to buy, you'll realise that the cover design is probably the most important factor in your decision-making process. It makes me want to cry when I see self-published books with amateur covers. You're a professional, so make sure your book looks like it is too; this means paying an experienced book cover designer to create one for you.

When you brief a designer consider the impression you want to make with your book. Are there brand colours to consider? What's the topic? Are there other book covers you admire which you'd like to emulate? What is it about them you like? Once you're clear on this, see if you can gain recommendations for cover designers from other authors, or go to a specialist design house. When you have a draft design through, consider how it will look at thumbnail size on the online bookstores. You'll be surprised at how large and clear the title has to be to read it, and how little room there is for other design features.

Back cover blurb

After the cover design, the wording on the back cover is the next element that sells a book to a potential reader if they're looking at it in a bricks-and-mortar store. Online, your blurb will provide inspiration for the promotional copy in your online listing. It should say who the book is for, what readers will learn from it, and a brief summary of the content. You also need to include a brief bio that explains what qualifies you to write it, together with a head shot. Your back cover can include a short testimonial, but only if it's from someone your readers have heard of.

Remember: people will look at your cover blurb to discover what's in it for them to read your book, and it's probably only *one thing*. I've seen many blurbs that go into too much detail in a desperate attempt to impress potential purchasers, who then end up feeling overwhelmed and confused. If they're not convinced by it, they won't buy it. What's the 'gold' in your book? Construct your blurb around that.

The technicalities

You know that barcode on the back of a book? That encodes its ISBN (International Standard Book Number), which identifies your book to the trade and allows sales tracking to take place. It's not compulsory to have one if you're self-publishing, but it's a good idea because you'll be able to provide verified sales figures if you need them. If you add the correct metadata into your ISBN,[1] you can also find that your book appears in online searches for people asking questions about your expertise. UK authors buy them from Nielsen, and in the USA from Bowker.[2]

Another technicality is the copyright notice you see on the first page of all books. There's no standard format for this but it's important to have it, so take a book you trust and base it on that if you like.

Finally, in the UK there's a legal requirement for you to submit a copy of your published book to the British Library and a small number of other libraries.[3]

Print and upload

In the old days, printing a book meant ordering a couple of thousand copies and stacking them in your garage. I

---

[1] Learn more about metadata at 'The Basics of Metadata', *IngramSpark*, www.help.ingramspark.com/hc/en-us/articles/115002276983-The-Basics-of-Metadata

[2] Nielsen, www.nielsenisbnstore.com/ and Bowker, www.bowker.com/products/ISBN-US.html

[3] Find out how to do this here: 'Legal Deposit', *British Library*, www.bl.uk/aboutus/legaldeposit/printedpubs/depositprintedpubs/deposit.html

remember my dad, an academic who self-published one of his many books, piling them up to the windowsill in his bedroom. Now, however, you can upload your files and have them turned into a professional book that's printed as each copy is ordered online – it's like magic. Amazon KDP and IngramSpark are the main services for this; KDP works well for selling books on the Amazon site, whereas IngramSpark is better for other retailers. There are pros and cons to each, and some authors choose to publish on both in order to take advantage of how they work; you can find information online to help you make an up-to-date decision.[4]

If you're publishing an e-book, either as a standalone or as an electronic version of a print book, you can simply upload the files and cover design onto the online retailers' platforms. That will almost certainly include Amazon's KDP. In my experience, it's best to have your e-book formatted in the correct file type before you upload it (save yourself some hassle by getting someone else to do it at low cost), and make sure you test it before it's published to check it reads as you expect.

Once your books are made flesh, use your back cover blurb to create your online sales descriptions. These are vital for attracting readers, and you need to make sure you've included the right keywords so your book is found in searches.

---

[4] Here's a helpful article that explains how it works: 'Why Indie Authors Should Use KDP Print & Ingramspark Together to Self-Publish Paperback Books', *ALLi*, www.selfpublishingadvice.org/kdp-print-ingram-spark-paperbacks/

Hybrid or partner publishing: what you need to know

When you work with a partner publisher, in some ways you have the best of both worlds. You don't endure the hassle of self-publishing but you do retain the control inherent in that route. However, choose your publishing partner wisely. Ask fellow authors for recommendations and speak to two or three providers. Apart from the obvious considerations such as costs and timings, here are some questions to ask.

- What experience do you have of the publishing industry?
- Can you send me samples of books you've published so I can see the quality?
- What royalties do you pay?
- What's the cost to me if I purchase author copies to sell or give away myself?
- Do I retain full control of my copyright?
- Do you create e-books and audio books?
- Are you able to get my book into bookstores and libraries?
- What marketing support do you offer?
- What editing and proof reading services are included?
- Can I talk to a couple of your authors to find out what they thought of working with you?

Any partner publisher worth working with will be more than happy to answer these questions, and many include a free session up front for you to talk about your book so they can advise you on the best publishing route. It really is one of those areas where the cheapest isn't necessarily the best, so make sure you feel you can work with them. They could turn out to be your most valuable supporter when your book is out.

Now your book is written and in the process of being published, you have permission to break open the bubbly. But wait – there's more. Your book won't sell itself, you know! It's time to think about marketing. The rest of this book is about how to sell or distribute as many copies of your book as your business needs, in order to achieve the goal you set yourself at the beginning. In walking you through this I'll be drawing on my 20 years' experience of traditional and online marketing before I became a ghostwriter and book coach. You'll enjoy the journey, I promise.

What we've covered

- ❖ There are three routes to publishing your book, each with their own pros and cons: traditional, self-, and hybrid or partner publishing.
- ❖ Traditional publishers will require a book proposal before they consider working with you.
- ❖ If you self-publish by doing everything yourself, you need to learn the stages of publishing.
- ❖ A hybrid publisher will project manage the task for you, for a fee.

III
PROMOTE

Chapter 14

How to market your book

Your promotional options

No story lives unless someone wants to listen.
JK Rowling

A coaching friend of mine, Julia, had the perfect experience when marketing her business book. Just before publication she sent a couple of emails to her professional network asking them to plug it, and posted a handful of tweets and posts online. To her amazement and delight, her book launched as an Amazon number one bestseller. In fact, after only a couple of days it had received over 30 five-star reviews and was being recommended far and wide. It virtually sold itself.

I'm sorry, but this never happens. I made it up.

In reality, the way most books are sold involves far more time and attention than that, although it can still be fun.

Lay your worries to rest

One of the concerns some people have about promoting their book is the feeling that they're drawing undue attention to themselves. This is compounded by the irrational fear so many of us labour under that our book is no good; that despite the expertise we've poured into it and the positive feedback we've received from editors and beta readers, we're frauds and shouldn't be allowed to call ourselves authors. Add to this, of course, the dislike of marketing felt by many a professional; give an HR or finance expert the choice between working with a client and promoting themselves, and I can guess which they'd prefer.

These are all understandable worries and can, of course, be resolved by the pulling up of the proverbial big girl or boy pants. However, I increasingly believe that underlying this state is the lack of tolerance we have for uncertainty. There are many things we know in life: that the sun will rise tomorrow, that our name won't change of its own accord, and that peas are green. But there are so many more we don't know, and we don't feel comfortable with that. So far your book's been under your control, but now it's about to fly into the world and you have unanswered questions. Will it sell? Who to? What will people think of it? Will it help your business? The truth is you don't know for sure, and that's okay – in fact, you can see it as part of the exciting journey you're about to embark on.

Some of your marketing will work and some of it won't, but it only takes one part of your campaign to light a fuse and you're off. Unless you try a range of options you'll never find out. What's more, one piece of activity can lead to another, bringing you results in a way you'd never have predicted at the beginning. So when you plot out your marketing strategy, build in some flexibility for not knowing exactly what will come of it. If you want 100% certainty in advance, the best advice I can give is not to do any marketing at all – that way, you'll be sure not to sell more than a few copies!

The good news is, marketing your book is a no-fail process because in the very act of doing it you'll be elevating your expert status, however many you do or don't sell. When you talk about your expertise and your book together, they make up more than the sum of their parts because having published a book is so impressive in its own right.

Where to start

From a practical point of view, there are two decisions you should make for your marketing:

- what you're going to do *before* you publish your book versus what you're going to do *after* it; and
- who you're going to market to in each of these phases.

Let's look at each phase in more detail.

Pre- versus post-publication marketing

I talked about pre-marketing in Chapter 4 so I won't go into more detail here, but I suggest you re-visit that chapter now to refresh your memory. Did you set up your author platform at that stage, and keep building it as you were writing? If you did, congratulations. If not there's no time to lose, so why not make a start right now. I'll take you through multiple online and offline options in the next two chapters so you can decide what's right for you.

Pre- versus post-publication audiences

In Chapter 11 you learned about why beta readers are important and how to use them, but after your book is published these people still have a role. They're your champions – the ones who already know your book, admire your knowledge, and are emotionally connected with what you're trying to achieve. What can you do to maximise their involvement? Could you send them a free copy and ask them to leave an honest review on Amazon? Craft personalised social media updates for them to use? Invite them to your book launch? Think of these people as your early adopters and make them feel special.

In addition to your small group of beta readers, you can also create a wider list of 20–30 people in your sphere of influence with whom you can develop a book marketing relationship. They could be individuals with a similar audience to yours but who aren't competitors; other experts you've teamed up with (or done favours for) in the past; friends; colleagues; clients (past and present); industry contacts; and anyone else you know will be on your side and happy to help you promote your book. Writing them down, together with their contact details, ensures nobody is forgotten.

As well as this select bunch you'll want to reach a much wider audience. Again, creating a list is helpful but this time not of individuals but of groups. Who can you identify? If your book is written for people interested in scientific research, for instance, your readership could consist of fellow scientists, a much broader group of people for whom it's an amateur interest, and students in the field. When you create your list, add a column next to each group identifying what marketing platforms each is likely to use. Scientists would read academic publications, attend conferences, and chat on professional forums, whereas consumers interested in science might participate in relevant social media groups, read blogs, and listen to certain podcasts. Where do the different groups of your audience hang out? What are their 'watering holes'?

Marketing polarities

In her excellent guide *How to Market a Book*, author Joanna Penn talks about what she calls 'marketing polarities'.[1] This is a helpful way of thinking about your book marketing because it shows you the breadth of options available. Here are those of Joanna's polarities that I consider to be most relevant to business authors, together with my thoughts on how they could relate to you.

---

[1] Joanna Penn, *How to Market a Book*, Createspace, 2013.

- *Short vs long term*: a concentrated burst of promotion at launch, or a steady stream of activity?

- *Paid vs free (or money vs time)*: are you willing to invest your time in building an audience long term, or are paid ads and placements the way to go?

- *Your first book when you have no ready-made audience vs subsequent books when you do*: do you have experience in what works for you, or are you trialling a variety of approaches for the first time?

- *Traditional vs self-publishing*: you have little choice about things like price, cover design, and title with the former, but with the latter you can do what you want and sell your book on your own website too.

- *Offline (could be global) vs offline (might be more local)*: the former is more scalable, but with the latter you can achieve a focused impact.

- *Introvert vs extrovert*: what suits you best – staying behind a keyboard or getting in front of (and mingling with) a crowd?

- *E-book vs print*: the former can only be marketed online, the latter you can sell at events and in person.

- *Data vs people focused*: the former involves keyword and category research, whereas the latter is more about speaking, blogging, and relationship building.

- *Push vs pull marketing*: push marketing is ads and other interruptive techniques, whereas pull marketing involves attraction and permission so your audience is drawn to you.

There's no right or wrong to any of these polarities, and it's also worth bearing in mind they're not mutually exclusive; you can do both short- and long-term marketing, for instance. But where I think these options are beneficial is how they enable you to narrow your decision-making. You could ask yourself:

- Which do I feel naturally drawn to?

- Which involve a learning curve and which could I get started with most quickly?

- Which are most relevant to the places my readers hang out?

Hone your marketing platform

Here's where you narrow in on where you will focus your marketing energies. I'm a fan of making your book marketing as fun and easy as possible, and that means tailoring your promotional activities to what's going to give you the biggest bang for your buck.

What do you love?

If you hate Facebook and are as attracted to public speaking as a dog to a bath, you're unlikely to stick with either of them long enough to have an effect. So focus on what you enjoy and have had success with in the past, leaving a little wiggle room for opportunities that come your way when you least expect them.

What do you already have?

If your blog is well loved and you enjoy writing it, that's an asset you can make use of to promote your book. If you have an email list with hundreds or thousands of names on it, you're well placed to spread your message far and wide through this channel. If your calendar is filled with speaking engagements, plan how you can work your book into your talks and sell them there. In other words, sweat your existing marketing assets first, because this is where they come into their own.

Try to make your marketing as friction-free as possible both for yourself and your readers. And while we're talking about making life easy, check back on Chapter 3 where you learned about streamlining your book marketing. Aligning your existing business audience with your book's potential readership is something not all business authors do, but it's the one thing that can make the difference between marketing being a hard slog that delivers few results, and it being relatively painless and effective.

So start with where you are now: What do you already do that a) gets results and b) could be adapted or extended to include marketing your book? If you're thinking of adding anything else, ask yourself if it's a good idea – it might be, but just be clear on why you're doing it.

And if you don't have a platform? I'm really sorry, but if that's the case you'll find it hard to sell your book. However, all is not lost because you almost certainly have more resources than you realise. When I coached one particular client through her book marketing options she was adamant she had no platform at all, but after delving into it she discovered she did have an audience – she just hadn't thought about it that way before. A quick brainstorm threw up over 50 people who could spread the word, and who she'd helped considerably over the years so they owed her a few favours; she had a nascent Twitter account that she could start to build up; and she could adapt her website to include a book page, complete with a link to Amazon and clips of video interviews about her topic.

Why chasing the bestseller lists may harm your prospects

I include this because I find many authors can get overly obsessed with numbers, rankings, and sales, and I'd like to save you some stress.

Before we dive in I need to explain there are, in a way, two kinds of nonfiction bestsellers. One is the type you see in the 'top reads' section of the chain bookstores or listed in the media such as *The Sunday Times*. These lists are populated by mainstream successes that appeal to broad audiences, and are usually on topics of wide interest with a compelling angle. They're almost always traditionally published. The other is the type that tops their Amazon categories; when sales rise enough to attain the number one spot, Amazon rewards them with a bestseller flag. These can be on more niche topics as the platform divides books into smaller groups; in fact, the more focused the book topic the more likely it is to achieve that status. Sales in a few of these categories can be relatively low but still be 'bestsellers'. Of course, the two types of bestseller can overlap, but it's helpful to know how it works.

Next, let's look at why book sales can be seen as such a big deal. The holy grail of the bestseller comes from the days when all books were produced by traditional publishers. Because of the up-front investment these publishers put into their books, they naturally focused on numbers so they could make as much profit as possible – in fact, they still do. The importance placed on sales figures led to a focus on bestseller charts, with authors and publishers basking in the shared glory of being at the top of the list (often achieved through expensive promotional efforts).

As I've described, this spotlight on rankings is also encouraged today by online sales platforms which constantly wave the book category sales positions in your face. Sometimes it can seem as if a book being a bestseller is all anyone talks about, leading you to assume that unless your book is one too, you may as well give up and go home. But as comedian Spike Milligan said when he pleaded, 'All I want is the chance to prove that money can't make me happy', selling piles of books isn't an automatic route to satisfaction. There's far more to it than that.

This is because although high sales are nice to have, they're rarely the primary reason a business book is written these days. You'll make the real returns through raising your profile and attracting more clients. How many copies do you need to sell in order to bring a queue of excited customers to your door? Only as many as it takes to put you in front of the right people. In fact, you may decide to give away a number of copies as a high-value business card.

However, there's also a more troubling side to the focus on achieving high sales, which is that it can even lead to you harming your book's success. That might sound extreme, but bear with me.

First of all, it can lead to you altering your target audience in an unhelpful way. Say you're a life coach specialising in helping divorced women in their 40s and 50s rebuild their lives, and your book is designed to position you as the go-to expert. You're fixated on it being a mainstream bestseller because you've heard how important that is, and anyway, who doesn't want to be top of the list? But your niche audience isn't broad enough to support thousands of sales, so you widen it to include all divorced women. That's a lot of people, and in so doing you've lost your focus on the specific issues they're facing at that time of their life. Now your book may turn out to be a bestseller or it may not, but even it if does hit the top of the rankings you'll not end up with the like-minded divorcée clients you're so good at helping; you've become known as more of a generalist. And that's not what you wanted out of your book, was it?

Secondly, co-ordinating a campaign to achieve bestseller status involves concentrated work which can be a distraction from your day-to-day business. Who knows what opportunities you may miss if you're spending every spare minute promoting your book during a two-week launch window? And what happens to sales in the months after that, when you're too exhausted and busy catching up to think about them?

Although it might seem like it, I'm not against having a bestseller – far from it. It can be a fantastic marketing message when your book tops the rankings. I'm just saying it's not worth neglecting the rest of your business or skewing your audience for, let alone feeling inadequate if you don't achieve it.

Going for bestseller status

Having said that, what should you do if you're determined to go for an online bestseller launch? You'll need to co-ordinate a concentrated marketing push around the time of publication so you sell as many copies as possible in a short space of time. That way, the algorithm picking up your sales pattern will push you towards the top of the list. Here are some ways you can encourage purchases at launch:

- Set up a page on your website telling your potential readers you'll send them special bonuses if they buy your book on a specific day. Ask them to go to Amazon, buy the book, then return to your web page and enter their purchase order number along with their email address. Then you can email them with their bonuses, such as tip sheets, video links, and additional material that will help them to get more out of the book. You'll also have their email addresses for future use.

- To encourage people to visit that page, email your list and all your relevant contacts ahead of time and on the day of launch. This is important, because you want them to be prepared to take action then and only then.

- Use social media to do the same. Broadcast a webinar or carry out other marketing activity specifically geared towards promoting sales on that day.

- Ask your core supporters to help you with this by publicising the launch on your behalf. If each one of them were to do the same as you, co-ordinating their efforts on the same day, think what you could achieve. Make this easy for them by creating a selection of email and social media wording templates, so all they have to do is copy and paste them onto their own platforms.

- Send a short series of two or three communications to these supporters in advance of your launch and also on the day. People are busy and have short memories, so leave nothing to chance.

- On the day, nervously cross your fingers and keep checking the rankings, erupting with joy if you hit the number one spot. Take a screenshot to prove it for posterity. Flagrantly boast about your achievement via every channel possible and collapse in an exhausted heap. Now you can call yourself a bestselling author – well done to you!

So far we've looked at what it means to market your book and how it works in overview. Next, we'll dive into the mechanics of book marketing both on- and offline.

What we've covered

❖ Try not to worry about putting yourself in the spotlight with your book – that's what it's for, after all.

❖ Your two main decisions are to decide how you'll promote your book pre- and post-publication, and who your audiences are in each phase.

❖ Make life easy for yourself by working with what you enjoy and what you already have.

❖ Achieving bestseller status isn't necessarily all it's cracked up to be, but there are ways of doing it if it's important to you.

Chapter 15

Marketing offline

The non-tech way of promoting your book

A survey shows that the number one fear of people is public speaking. Number two is death. That means that at a funeral the average person would rather be in the casket than doing the eulogy.
Jerry Seinfeld

It may seem artificial to break marketing into offline and online activities because they're both aimed at making the right people aware of your book, wherever they hang out. However, there is sense in it. For a start, offline marketing usually involves longer lead times than online, as well as requiring different skills and considerations. What's more, breaking up marketing into two areas makes the topic easier to digest – never a bad thing.

In both the off- and online chapters I'll explain how each element of marketing works, together with their pros and cons. Of course, what I see as an advantage you may see as a drawback and vice versa; 'different strokes for different folks', as the saying goes. But that's okay – the main outcome I want is for you to decide what you're going to do. Treat the options as a smorgasbord of what's on offer, helping yourself to whatever appeals most. Take care not to make it an all you can eat buffet, though, or you'll end up with marketing indigestion.

Offline marketing is what you might think of as 'traditional' marketing. It's the old-fashioned kind where you meet people face to face or promote yourself via print media, just like you would have done 20 years ago. It's all the more charming for it in my view, but that's not to say it has any inherent advantage; it's just an alternative way of marketing your business and your book rather than via the Internet.

The advantages of offline

Some business owners feel more comfortable with offline marketing than online. You don't need to set up accounts or manage the intricacies of social media, and there's something blissfully straightforward about it. If this is how you're used to doing business and it works for you, then make the most of it because offline promotion also gives you the chance to physically present your book to people when you meet them, which has a powerful effect.

It does have its limitations, though. There's a ceiling on the number of people you can meet offline (even if you're talking to a packed conference room), and when you want to sell large numbers of a promotional item – which is what your book is – there are only so many you can flog at one event.

Here are each of the main offline promotional options in turn, together with their pros and cons. This should help you decide which to focus on.

PR in print, TV, and radio

When people think about book marketing, often what they have in mind is PR. Offline, this can take different forms: print media articles, interviews, book reviews, and TV and radio interviews. I have mixed feelings about spending too much time on these, because you need to consider whether they're going to lead to more sales. Print, TV, and radio media tend to be consumed away from the most convenient place to buy your book, which is on a computer or other device. If your potential book buyers read about you in a magazine while they're sitting in a tunnel on the London Underground, the chances are they'll have forgotten by the time they surface into the land of connectivity; even if they don't, there's no handy link to click on. This isn't the case, of course, for online PR.

What effective PR can give you, though, is fantastic exposure for your business especially if you promote the fact that you've appeared on a high-value media outlet. In this sense, your book is your excuse to talk to a journalist about what you do. How many times do you watch a chat show only to discover the main guest has just published a book. Strange coincidence, isn't it?

What do you need in order to generate some PR? All journalists want an angle, preferably a topical one. What current issues could your book relate to? Is there an emotional, human element to them? The more up to date, controversial, emotionally-driven, and personal your hook is the better. And be ready to be quick to respond: following the hashtag #journorequest on Twitter can be an excellent way to find out about what's going on. It's used by journalists in all fields who want people to interview on their topic, and that person could be you.

You've probably heard about press releases and how they're essential for launching your book in the media, and it's true, journalists do use them when they're deciding what to write about. There are various online resources you can use to learn how to write one,[1] but you may choose to hire a PR professional for crafting your release and contacting publications on your behalf. There's a lot of legwork involved in getting your book noticed by the media, and you probably won't have the time or resilience for it yourself. However, you can also use your personal connections to reach relevant writers and interviewers, and keep an eye out for opportunities. Landing an expert interview is often just a matter of being in the right place at the right time.

---

[1] 'How to Write a Press Release for a Book Launch', *Made for Success Publishing*, www.madeforsuccess.com/uncategorized/how-to-write-a-press-release-for-a-book-launch/

PR pros

- An amazing way of promoting your business, if you use your book as the hook for the interview or article that puts you in the spotlight
- Some media have huge audiences
- It's free (unless you hire a PR expert)

PR cons

- Coverage isn't guaranteed
- It isn't the best platform for driving book sales
- It can be time consuming and frustrating

Speaking at events

When I was first asked to give a talk about how to write a business book, I used the bare bones of this book to create it. Naturally I put the information across in a different way than I've done here, but it was useful to have it as a starting point and it meant I ended up saying 'yes' to a speaking opportunity I might have otherwise assumed would be too much work. This shows how having a book and being a speaker can be symbiotically useful. Your book can form the basis of your talks, and you'll be far more attractive to a speaker booker once you're an author. One of my ghostwriting clients told me he was able to add an extra couple of thousand pounds to his speaking fees once his book was published.

If you're a speaker – whether professional or occasional – how can you use your talks to promote your book? One way is to sell copies of it at events you speak at, as long as the organisers allow; some speakers even negotiate a certain number of copies to be bought as part of their fee. Another way is to always be thinking about how you can bring your book into your speaking. The next time you have the chance to be filmed doing a talk, make sure you hold your up book to the audience and insert some footage of this into your show reel. Or how about being interviewed on your book topic, and creating a series of videos of the process? Through this you'll build your book into the marketing you're already doing for your speaking career.

Whenever you receive a booking enquiry, send them a copy of your book. A tip one professional speaker gave me is to pop a sticky note on the cover suggesting the most relevant chapter for them to look at, given the topic of the talk they're suggesting. Reading your book gives your enquirer a feel for your tone of voice and approach – they're able to know, like, and trust you before you've even met.

Speaking pros

- If you're speaking anyway, it makes sense to use your platform to promote your book
- You can sell copies of your book at the events where you're speaking
- Arranging speaking opportunities to audiences that are relevant to your book is an excellent way to put it in front of people

Speaking cons

- You can only speak to so many people at once
- If you're not skilled and experienced as a speaker there's a learning curve to becoming proficient, and you might not want to embark on this just to promote your book

Networking

If you already take part in face-to-face networking for your business, it makes superb sense to bring a few copies of your book along with you. A book is the ultimate business card because it says more about you and your expertise than anything else could. If you develop a rapport with someone who seems interested in how you can help them, offer them a free copy or send it along afterwards (thereby providing the ideal excuse to follow up).

Networking pros

- Presenting your book face to face is highly impactful
- A book is more effective than a business card

Networking cons

- You'll only meet a limited number of people at one time

Book launch party

There can be no more watertight an excuse for a party than having just published a book. If you can't reserve a venue, lay on some drinks, and summon your friends and family on this momentous occasion, when can you? Throwing a launch party is by no means essential but if you're the sociable type it's an enjoyable way of cementing your business relationships, building new ones, and promoting your book. Personally I would rather eat my book page by page than throw a party, but that's because I hate being the centre of attention in a crowded room. If you feel comfortable with the idea, though, go ahead and be my guest (or rather, I'll be yours).

Before you place that wine order, though, you need to work out why you're having a launch do in the first place. Here are the top reasons to throw one, and yours may be a combination of all four:

- to celebrate the results of your hard work with friends and family;
- to reward and network with the professionals and supporters who've helped you on your book journey;
- to gain PR for your book; and
- to sell copies of your book at the event.

Let's unpick this. A party that's primarily designed to appeal to your friends and family is unlikely to bring in many influential journalists for PR. Journalists generally require a daytime event at a location that's easy to reach, whereas your loved ones might prefer an evening do at a location closer to where they live. You'll also need to bear in mind that journalists have a reputation for saying they'll turn up and then reneging at the last minute. They need a solid reason for thinking your book launch is the kind of newsworthy event they can squeeze a few hundred words out of, and the reality is that most of the time it isn't. You might attract a local journalist or two, or someone who writes for a publication with a specialist interest in your niche, but you'd probably have as much luck sending them a copy of your book and asking them to review it.

Where a book launch can definitely help to promote your book, however, is if you use it as a way of rewarding everyone who's helped you with it. These are the people you want to keep on your side – your core helpers. Bringing them together in a physical space is a tangible way of thanking them, and also of helping them to extend their own networks. To encourage them to attend, ask yourself what they would gain from attending your launch. Can you offer them a chance to hobnob with influential guests, and with each other? What's in it for them? One of my ghostwriting clients invited a high-profile media presenter to interview her at her launch; it was an effective way of raising awareness of the book and attracting people to come at the same time.

For your venue, choose somewhere appropriate in size and budget. You may find a local cafe or hotel will offer a free space as long as you buy the drinks and snacks from them, but be prepared to pay if you want somewhere special. It's also a good idea to allow time for networking (you're thinking about what your attendees want, remember). A short talk, with maybe a reading from your book, is the usual thing to do, as is a question and answer session afterwards. And at some point you need to allow time for book signing. That's where a photographer comes in handy – there's no better ego boost than a shot of you signing a pile of books at your very own party!

There are also ways to think of your launch event as being more than just about your book; it can promote your business, too. Any PR or photos and video footage can be used on social media and your website, and if you can work in some local radio or press PR around the event all the better. Leverage the value for all you're worth.

You'll need to have loads of books to sign and sell, along with a table to display them on and a mechanism for taking payment. Afterwards, follow up with your guests to thank them and ask them to share pictures on social media. You can also nudge them to review your book online.

Book launch party pros

- They're great fun if you love a party
- They're useful for networking and cementing your business relationships
- You can use the assets from the event to promote your book on social media and your website

Book launch party cons

- They can be expensive and time-consuming to organise
- You may expect more PR than you'll receive
- They're not a money-making venture in their own right

Conferences and events

Whether you're an attendee, a speaker, or an exhibitor, a conference is one of the most time-honoured ways of meeting a whole host of people who share your professional interest. There are multiple ways of putting your book in front of people at an event. You can take a stand to exhibit and sell it, put yourself forward as a speaker, or simply mingle with the crowds and treat it as a large networking event (although this is less effective). Also, ask if the event organiser is giving away goodie bags because your book might be a worthwhile addition to it.

As an example of how exhibiting can work, a ghostwriting client of mine sent stand invitations to selected prospects ahead of an event. Included was the chance to pick up a free, signed copy of her book, as well as to be entered into a competition to win an additional prize. She even managed to have a photo taken of her holding her book with a visiting politician while she was there. The result was a queue of people waiting to see her, which generated valuable new business.

Conferences and events pros

- If you'll be at the event anyway, your book can add value to your presence
- If you're targeted about it, you can use it as a way of introducing yourself to potential clients
- Speaking at an event is a brilliant way of explaining the value of your book

Conferences and events cons

- Events are time-consuming and can be expensive to exhibit at or attend
- While you come into contact with more people than at a networking event, your numbers are limited by those you can manage to talk to

Entering your book for an award

This is something that doesn't occur to many business authors, but it's too good an opportunity to miss. The prestige of being able to call yourself an award-winning author is immense, and a huge boost to your confidence as well. I've been a judge myself for the Business Book Awards, which gave me a behind-the-scenes peek into how these events operate. All awards are run differently but often your book will be judged according both to the information you provide when you submit it, and on the book itself. This means it's vital to have a compelling pitch to hand, which if you did your planning before you wrote your book will be simple.

How do you enter your book for an award?

1. *Decide which awards to enter* (some prohibit you from entering more than one at once, so bear this in mind). Examples of worthwhile nonfiction awards are: The Business Book Awards, the FT & McKinsey Business Book of the Year Award, Axiom Business Book Awards, the 800-CEO-READ Business Book Awards, CMI Management Book of the Year, the Small Business Book Awards, and APEX Awards for Publication Excellence. Criteria to guide your choice should include the specific rules for entry, whether or not the awards contain a suitable category for your book, and whether the audience for the awards aligns with that of your book.

2. *Check the entry requirements* thoroughly so you understand the implications of entering.

3. *Craft a compelling and concise entry wording.* This will depend on the individual awards requirements.

4. *Enter and keep your fingers crossed.* You could at least send your best suit or dress to the dry cleaners.

If you're lucky enough to win a spot on the shortlist make the most of this on social media, your email list, your website, and your Amazon description. If you *win* a category, or even the whole competition, you've struck marketing gold and have full permission to go wild on the publicity (let's face it, you're probably going to go wild anyway so you may as well sell some books while you're about it). You'll also find the company running the awards will be delighted to help you promote your win, as that provides reciprocal publicity. Most awards will give you a winner's badge design to put on your book cover, so be sure to add it on.

Awards pros

- Fantastic for credibility if you're shortlisted or win
- The awards ceremony (if there is one) is a great networking opportunity
- Your book will receive a sales boost if you do well

Awards cons

- Can be time-consuming and (in a few cases) expensive to enter
- Your book's fate is in the lap of the gods

What we've covered

- ❖ The wonderful thing about offline marketing is how personal it is – you have the chance to talk to people face to face about your book.
- ❖ It has the disadvantage of being limited in scope and is also not an effective way to sell books online.
- ❖ The main offline channels are PR, speaking, networking, book launch parties, conferences, and awards. Each has its own pros and cons.

Chapter 16

Marketing online

Using your website and social media to promote your book

To err is human, but to really foul things up you need a computer.
Paul R. Ehrlich, American biologist

Online marketing has the power to amplify whatever you say or do (hence the good-humoured warning embedded in the quote above). I love it, but then I'm a writer and sitting at my desk is my idea of heaven. What's more, I worked for several years as a social media manager, shaping and managing the online presence of all sorts of companies. My experience with this benefits you two ways: if you're more of an offline marketing fan you'll have much to learn from this chapter, and if you're an online-lover like me you're bound to discover something you've not thought of before.

The advantages of online

Think of the online world as a vast city populated by millions of people; its reach is almost infinite and you can wander its streets without even leaving the comfort of your chair. Of those millions there will be thousands whose hopes and dreams your book can help to fulfil. Pretty tempting, yes? However, if those digital highways are simple for you to access, they're equally as easy for anyone else who's promoting a book. So you need to design an identity for yourself that's special to you, and aim your messages at an audience that's small enough for you to build an effective relationship with.

In other words, while offline you can get away with being somewhat generalised about what you do because you have the chance to build face-to-face relationships that make you memorable ('I'm a life coach'), in the online space you're afforded no such luxury. If your potential buyers aren't instantly grabbed by your compelling marketing message, your competitors' books are only a click away. Your book must stand out like a gleaming skyscraper in Internet City, and this chapter explains how.

Your website

I'm assuming you already have a website for your business, and rarely is there a need to create a separate one for your book. In fact, it's usually better to promote your book on your existing site so each shares its marketing juice with the other. People viewing your website will be doubly convinced of your authority because not only are you showcasing your expertise on there, it's clear you've written a book about it too.

As a minimum, create a new page on your site to feature your book. If you use the right keywords in your page title and content, this will help people to stumble across your book when they're Googling for advice on your area – they might not even be looking for a book but they'll come across it that way. Include a picture of the cover (you can find someone online to create a 3D one at a low cost), who it's for, what unique and timely advice or information it offers, and the knowledge your potential readers will gain from reading it. How will their lives be different? What's in it for them? This is also the place to include a link to buy it; if you're selling it on your own site you can run special offers to tempt people.

However, the value of your website doesn't stop at promoting your book. You can also use it to give your readers extra resources, thereby bolstering the value of the book for them. If you 'gate' these resources behind an email address, you have the added bonus of being able to carry on an online conversation long term. We talked earlier about lead magnets in your book, and here are a couple of further ideas which link to this concept in a more substantial format than a simple pdf or video.

- *Diagnostic quiz.* Does your book contain an element of 'are you this kind of business or person?' If so, an interactive quiz on your site can be a help to your readers. You can also learn a lot from the results; one of my clients discovered her readers were far less clued up in a particular area than she'd assumed, so she used this knowledge to inform her workshops and also her next book.

- *Book resource page.* If you have a number of resources in your book to offer your readers, you can collect them into one page on your site called www.yourdomain/bookresources (or similar). This is where you place links to the downloads and videos you mention in the book, and remember to add the requirement to enter an email address in order to access them. I'll go into how you can use those emails in a moment.

Website pros

- You already have one so it makes sense to promote your book on it

- You can use the technology however you like

- You can add marketing elements one by one, or in one go – it's up to you

Website cons

- Depending on your website platform and level of technical skill, you may have to spend a bit of money on making the changes you want. I'd recommend a WordPress site, to which you can add plug-ins to provide the functions you need.

Your blog

In a way, a business book is a bit like a huge, structured blog. Both are geared towards a specific audience, both impart useful and inspiring information, and both aim to change their readers' lives or work for the better. The differences are that a blog does this in bite-sized chunks and is updateable after publication, whereas a book delivers the whole shebang in one go and is 'forever'. It follows from this that your blog is an ideal place to promote your book, and also that by writing your book you've already generated much of the blog content you need.

There are many ways to approach writing a blog post. You can create a 'how-to' post; interview an expert with a similar audience to you and write it up; craft an 'all you can eat' post which explains a topic from your book in depth; or come out with a controversial or manifesto piece that highlights your special take on your subject.

In addition to the above, try these ideas:

- create a series of blog posts based on your book's content, mentioning your book during each post and at the end (with a link to where people can buy it);

- curate a list of books similar to yours and include yours in it, giving honest reviews;

- ask any contributors to your book, or experts who've helped you to promote it, to write a guest post for your blog (they'll want to promote the post to their audience as well); and

- film a series of videos talking about various elements of your book, hosting them on your YouTube channel and embedding them into your blog.

Blogging pros

- If you set it up on your website you're utilising an existing asset for free
- It brings traffic to your site
- You can re-purpose content from your book

Blogging cons

- It takes time
- Blogging requires a different approach to that of writing a book, as you need to be mindful of grabbing attention rather than sustaining reader interest over a longer period

Your email list

There are two ways I'll talk about your email list. The first is to use it to sell your book, the second is to keep the conversation going with your readers once they've bought it. Let's look at the second one first.

Imagine this offline scenario. You own a delicatessen, with some of your customers returning repeatedly (the regulars) and others dropping by occasionally (the casuals). To reward the regulars, you make a point of chatting with them whenever they come in.

'How are you today, Mrs Jones?' you ask. 'After your usual cured ham? We're stocking a new variety this week.'

'Oh fine', Mrs Jones replies. 'I'm just in for one of your delicious cheeses but I'll come by tomorrow and try the ham. My husband might pop in too, he loves that kind of thing.'

'That's great, looking forward to seeing you. We'll have a tasting for our artisan chutney range then too.'

While you've been chatting a couple of casual customers have come in, had a look around, and just as quickly popped out again. You see the value of the regulars? They're more loyal, more lucrative, and are more likely to recommend you – and it makes no difference whether it's a bricks-and-mortar store or an online business. In the same way, your book readers are casuals at first and your aim is to turn at least some of them into regulars. The best method of doing that is to keep in touch with them. Email is the ideal digital method for turning a one-off, transactional relationship (the buying of your book) into a long-term one, because you have the chance to talk to your audience on a regular basis, just like you would with your customers if you owned a store.

If you already send a regular email to your target audience you're in a great position, because the lead magnets in your book will increase your list and allow you to expand your activity. And if emailing is foreign to you, now's the ideal time to consider it. Your aim is to distribute regular, interesting, and informative content that showcases your expertise. Being helpful and knowledgeable is a huge asset, and will set you apart from many other authors. Then, when it comes to launching a programme, recruiting new clients, or even selling your next book, you'll have a ready-made audience. It's so worth the effort and it's a lovely way to obtain feedback on your work and ideas, too.

To do this you'll need an account with a marketing email provider such as MailChimp, AWeber, Constant Contact, or ConvertKit – the list grows all the time, so it's worth exploring the most up-to-date options for your needs. Most offer a free version to try out, but investing a small amount for the professional level will pay dividends as you'll be able to make more of the service. Aim to send an email at least once a month, and weekly if you can. Why not link to your latest blog post, bring news of what's happening in your readers' industries, or share any thoughts and experiences that would be relevant to them? Also, just like in your book, you want to bring out your personality. You've had plenty of practice talking about your ideas persuasively and with clarity by now, so it should be easy to translate that into an email newsletter.

Now let's look at using your email list to sell your book. When you have a regular email up and running, it makes perfect sense to use it to market your book – however small the list. Think of the two main options:

- whipping up interest and sales by generating excitement about it; and

- encouraging book sales longer term through pull-outs of the book's key points or by offering discounts and incentives.

In terms of timing, you can use your list both to create a buzz at launch and as an ongoing promotional drip. Even just telling your recipients you've written a book will be a credibility builder in its own right; you'll probably see a surge in sales for your services along with those for your book.

Email pros

- You own your email list, unlike your social media platforms – no one can take it from you
- It enables you to build a long-term relationship with your readers
- Emailing is a direct and effective way to sell your book (and services)
- It's low tech, low cost, and easy to use
- It's flexible

Email cons

- It takes time and commitment to send a regular email newsletter
- If you don't keep it up your list will go 'cold' and you'll find it hard to generate interest in the future

Social media

I often think the world is divided into two sets of people: those whose eyes light up when they hear the words 'social media' and those whose eyes roll. What are you – a lighter or a roller? If you're the latter, this part of the book isn't intended to pull you over to the dark side; when I said the marketing that works is the marketing you want to do, I meant it. But why not give it a read anyway, in case there's a nugget in here that prompts you to re-evaluate social media? And if you're a lighter, read on.

An important point about social media: it's not a quick fix. You need to spend time building connections, engaging with them, and posting content that's useful and interesting before you see results; this takes several months at a minimum. The following assumes you've already built a presence or are willing to spend time doing so. Another piece of advice is not to use social media to sell overtly, as this will turn people off. Instead, build relationships and find indirect ways to sell your book – I'll explain how in the platform-by-platform section below.

At the time of writing, mainstream social media for business is made up of a relatively small number of platforms: LinkedIn, Twitter, Facebook, and YouTube. Some people include Instagram too, although I'll not go into it here as it's only useful for certain types of businesses. Drawing on my previous experience as a social media manager for companies, here are some practical suggestions for how you could use them to market your book.

LinkedIn

Many dismiss this as dull and boring, but it can be pretty exciting when you gain attention for your book on it. Try these tips:

- add 'author' to the headline on your profile;

- mention your book and how it helps people in your profile summary;

- put a promotional image of your book in the banner area at the top of your profile;

- write a series of articles about topics in your book, linking to your book's page on your website (or Amazon) at the end; and

- create a post to announce your book's publication, with a link to where people can buy it.

If nothing else, talking about yourself as a business author on LinkedIn will boost your authority on the site. See everything else as a bonus.

Twitter

You can have a lot of fun with Twitter, and the nature of the platform lends itself to repeated messages and content posting. Try these ideas:

- add 'author' (together with your book title, if you have enough space) to your bio for instant credibility, and put your book on your profile header image;

- schedule a series of posts announcing your book's launch, together with an eye-catching image and a link to where people can place pre-orders; and

- tweet a series of blog posts which focus on your book's topics.

Facebook

For many business authors, Facebook isn't a great platform as it's geared more to personal content than to business. But it depends. Many authors have built considerable followings on it, either via their personal profiles or their business pages (or both), and if you've done this it's definitely a good idea to talk about your book on there. The same goes if you're in Facebook groups where your book audience hangs out. Here's how:

- build anticipation by posting your book cover names and choices, and asking for feedback;

- announce your book's publication, together with how excited you are about it (remember Facebook is personal, so give it a friendly slant); and

- talk about any special offers you have on your book from time to time, but especially at launch.

YouTube

You'll either love or hate the thought of putting yourself on YouTube. It's important because it's the second largest search engine to Google, so when people search for the topic your book is about they may well come across your videos. For that reason alone, it can't be ignored. Try these ideas:

- if you're a speaker, create some video footage of you holding up your book and talking about it on stage, then post it online;

- film yourself talking about why you wrote the book and what's in it for your readers, adding a link to buy it high up in the video description; and

- create a series of videos based on different chapters of your book. Can you visualise your book content in such a way that a video would add to it?

Social media pros

- It's free

- You can reach a huge audience

- It gives you the opportunity to cultivate business relationships both long and short term

Social media cons

- It takes time to build an audience, make connections, and create a presence

- You won't achieve results just by posting – engagement with your followers is just as important, and this takes time and effort

- You need to keep at it regularly

Podcasts and online summits

Being interviewed on someone's podcast or online summit is an excellent way of positioning yourself as the go-to authority on your topic, and can link beautifully with promoting your book. If you're not sure what online summits are, they're online conferences hosted around a particular topic which pull in guest speakers in separate interviews. I've appeared on several podcasts and summits over the years and can testify to their effectiveness in gaining exposure – several potential clients have mentioned that they first heard of me when they listened to them. They're also far less scary than you may think.

Being interviewed gives you the freedom to talk about your book and your expertise by basing your answers around your book's topic as much as possible. You also have ready access to the interviewer's audience, so it's worth making sure it's a similar one to your own. Usually the show will include online notes where you can include your bio – make sure you include a lead magnet or a link to your book so you can capture email addresses or book sales.

You can search for summits and podcasts via Google and Twitter, or you can invite yourself onto a summit that's coming up – they may still welcome new speakers. I've done that myself and was inserted into the schedule at short notice when someone else let the organiser down. When the show is live, promote it on your own platforms, thereby selling copies of your book and increasing your expert credibility.

You can, of course, set up your own podcast or even host your own online summit. If you build it around the theme of your book it can be incredibly effective as a sales tool and authority builder in one. Publisher Alison Jones even launched a podcast to encourage her publicly to write her own business book, *This Book Means Business*, and over a hundred episodes later it's still going strong.[1] You never know what can happen …

Podcasts and summits pros

- They give you the chance to reach (potentially) thousands of listeners and viewers

- You can promote your interview via your own social channels as well as relying on your host to do the same, thereby increasing your audience

- You're able to build a relationship with your hosts, extending your professional network

- Setting up your own podcast or summit enables you to build your marketing platform still further

Podcasts and summits cons

- You're reliant on others to agree to interview you

- If you're setting up your own podcast or summit this is a considerable amount of work, with a significant learning curve

---

[1] Alison Jones, *This Book Means Business: Clever Ways to Plan and Write a Book That Works Harder for Your Business*, Practical Inspiration, 2018. You can find Alison's podcast (Episode 108) here: www. extraordinarybusinessbooks.com/category/podcast/

What we've covered

❖ The main advantage of marketing your book online is the huge reach available to you, coupled with the ability to provide links so people can buy your book instantly.

❖ This is also your major challenge, as you'll be competing with thousands of other authors.

❖ The main online channels are your website, blog, and social media platforms, and also summits and podcasts. Each has its own pros and cons.

Chapter 17

Become an authority with your book

A book can enrich your business

Writing [books] is perhaps the greatest of human inventions,
binding together people, citizens of distant epochs, who never
knew one another. Books break the shackles of time – proof
that humans can work magic.
Carl Sagan, science communicator

If you're like most business owners, the main reason you're
writing a book is to give yourself more authority. In fact,
the term itself comes from the word 'author'. To me, it
means being the originator of ideas and concepts that make
a difference to the world (or even a tiny part of it). To
become an authority you need to have worthwhile things
to say, communicate them so they're appreciated and

understood, and be able to command the attention of an audience that wants to hear about them.

It's this audience we've been looking at in Part III, 'Promote', because to effect change your message needs to be known, and this involves you standing out. Some people will be drawn to you and will want to work with you as a result. Others won't agree with you or might even dislike you for what you have to say, but there's no way around it: if you want to be considered an authority you should be willing to put yourself on a podium and allow the spotlight to shine on you. That doesn't mean being a show-off, but it does entail having a level of confidence in your point of view and a willingness to defend it.

Where does your book come into this? It's hard to think of many experts who are widely considered as authorities in their field who aren't also authors. This is because there's something magical about a book: it proves you know enough about your area of expertise to write a huge chunk of words on it. Words that motivate, inspire, and educate. That's impressive.

Conduct a celebrity marriage

When you're giving your business the support and authority that only a book can bring, that's not as far as it goes – you can also use your book to add an extra dimension to your business. It's like when Spice Girl Victoria Adams married David Beckham – together they became greater than the sum of their parts.

Earlier I talked about how the process of writing a book prompts you to think more deeply about your expertise, helping you to come up with ideas, frameworks, and lines of thought that enrich the way you work. This might take the form of creating new ways of helping people, and here are some examples.

Online courses

By creating a structure for your knowledge in the form of a book, you're ideally placed to turn it into a series of training modules. You can sell these separately or include them for your one-to-one clients, so they're able to hit the ground running when they start working with you.

Workbooks

If your book is a how-to guide, creating a companion workbook for it can be helpful for your readers. Many authors who do this offer it as a free download in exchange for an email address within the book, enabling them to communicate with their readers long term. For a brilliant example of someone who's done this successfully, see what Bryony Thomas has achieved with her book *Watertight Marketing*.[1] Readers who register their copy with her receive a set of workbooks and templates, access to a Facebook group, invitations to monthly masterclasses, and the option to buy into her marketing programmes to help them implement what they've learned in the book. You

---

[1] 'Your Essential Manual for Confident Marketing Decisions', *Watertight Marketing*, www.watertightmarketing.com/toolkit/about-the-book/

can see how she's made her business and her book work together.

Mini editions

You could create a cut-down version of your book to sell in bulk, especially if you speak at large events. These can be sold for a lower price than the full version or given away for free, and they're an extra way of capturing attention. To reduce your book in scope, consider taking a section from your original or an excerpt from it – anything from 40–100 pages (think of how the big-name publishers are doing this now, such as for the Dummies series). You could strike a deal with the organiser of an event to include the mini books in their goody bags, or with a company that has an audience similar to yours for them to slip into their physical mailouts. The most enthusiastic of your readers are bound to want the full version, and may go on to buy it. This is a trend that's starting to grow, so it's worth keeping an eye on anyone you see doing it and using your imagination about how it could work for you.

What we've covered

❖ Becoming an author gives you the power to spread your ideas and advice.

❖ You can use your book to develop extra assets for your business, thereby creating a symbiotic relationship between your book and your expertise.

The final chapter

Make the most of your new author status

> *No surprise in the writer, no surprise in the reader.*
> Robert Frost

Whenever I ask someone who's just published their book whether the experience was as they thought it would be, I'm met with incredulity.

> *It took me so much longer than I thought.*

> *Oh, it was hard!*

(or more positively...)

> *I never realised I knew all this stuff.*

> *It's so exciting now it's finished, I'm already thinking about my next one.*

The range of reactions is as diverse as the authors themselves. Some revel in the ideas they've generated, others in the opportunities coming their way now that their name is widely known. Most are surprised by what they've learned about themselves, which is brilliant – we should never stop impressing ourselves whenever we have the chance.

For myself, writing this book has been transformative. I've delved deeper into my processes and ideas than I've ever done before, I've gained the satisfaction of pulling my scattered pieces of wisdom into one permanent place, and I'm excited about what will happen after it's published. Who might stumble across it and read it? What doors will it open? And how many business books will now come into the world that would have stayed in their authors' heads had it not been for this one? It's enough to make a person glow.

So given the mountain you've just climbed, what does the future hold now you have a book in your name, apart from being able to sit back with a satisfied grin and say, 'I did it'?

For starters, you join a club. A group of people who have the knowledge, sticking power, and vision not only to dream of writing a book but to complete it. One consultant told me how fun it was to swap book stories with other business authors, and to feel for the first time that she was on an equal footing with them.

Secondly, be prepared for exciting opportunities to come your way. These can be as serendipitous as an influencer reading your book and asking you to appear on their podcast (which someone listens to who later becomes a valued client). Or it could be that you touch the lives of people who then recommend you to their friends. One thing's for sure, your reach will become more global than it was before, because once your book's available to buy online there are no territorial barriers to anyone hearing about you.

And finally, there's the emotional satisfaction. One of my ghostwriting clients told me how overwhelmed she felt when random people at conferences would come up and tell her how much they'd enjoyed her book. Another met someone who'd read his book and made significant changes to the way he led his life – the ultimate reason for the author writing it in the first place. Also, gaining more confidence in your subject and your ability to be unstoppable is an enormous boost, as is the tummy-tingling jolt of joy you feel when you realise you're becoming known as 'the person who wrote…'

There are some adjustments to make, though. Remember when we talked about your return on investment for your book? Think about what this means for you. Could it be that you can increase your prices (yes!), seek out a higher level of speaking gig so you're talking to larger audiences, or raise your sights when it comes to the clients and customers you aim at? This is a conscious process, because it's easy to stay in the 'what I think I'm worth' rut. Now you're published you have a special status, so make the most of it.

And above all, enjoy being a business author. It's all it's cracked up to be, I promise.

The author

Ginny Carter is a nonfiction book ghostwriter and writing coach. She has ghosted books on a wide variety of topics, from HR to phobias, some of which have been taken on by major publishing houses. They all have one thing in common: they're bringing their authors visibility, credibility, and bookability. She's also the author of the award-winning e-book *The Business Book Outline Builder*, which lays out the five key steps for creating the perfect outline.

Communication has always been Ginny's thing – she worked in marketing for 21 years, including three years as a freelance social media manager. By posting and tweeting on behalf of her clients she learned how gifted she was at capturing their voices. So she decided to put her natural writing ability to more substantial use and help them write their books instead.

When she can be dragged away from her keyboard, she puts her communication skills to the ultimate test with her husband and two children in their canalside home in Macclesfield, UK. Either that, or she has her nose in a brilliant book.

If you have a book waiting to emerge but aren't sure where to begin, or whether you have the time to devote to it, please start a conversation by dropping her a line using one of the links below:

Website: www.marketingtwentyone.co.uk

LinkedIn: www.linkedin.com/in/ginnycarter

Twitter: @_GinnyCarter

Here's to your book!

Further resources

Here are some other books about writing, publishing, and marketing – I've picked ones that are especially relevant for a business book.

~

The Business Book Outline Builder, Ginny Carter
This Book Means Business, Alison Jones
How to Write Your Book Without the Fuss, Lucy McCarraher and Joe Gregory
Write to the Point, Sam Leith
The Storytelling Toolkit, Lynda McDaniel and Virginia McCullough
Wired for Story, Lisa Cron
The Tall Lady with the Iceberg, Anne Miller
Dictate Your Book, Monica Leonelle
Quick Cheats for Writing with Dragon, Scott Baker
Successful Self-Publishing, Joanna Penn
The Authority Guide to Publishing Your Business Book, Sue Richardson
Write the Perfect Book Proposal, Jeff Herman and Deborah Levine Herman
Writers' & Artists' Yearbook

How to Market a Book, Joanna Penn
Book Marketing Made Simple, Karen Williams

Here are some blogs and podcasts you might also want to subscribe to as part of your business book writing journey.

Ginny Carter: www.marketingtwentyone.co.uk/articles (my own blog)
The Creative Penn: www.thecreativepenn.com/blog
Jane Friedman: www.janefriedman.com/blog
The Extraordinary Business Book Club Podcast: www.extraordinarybusinessbooks.com/podcast-episodes
The Creative Penn Podcast: www.thecreativepenn.com/podcasts
The Bestseller Experiment Podcast: www.bestsellerexperiment.com/podcasts

Acknowledgements

First let me thank my beta readers – the supportive friends and colleagues who read and gave feedback on this book before it was finalised. Your constructive criticism and supportive comments made all the difference. Alison Jones, James, Crow, Julie Dennis, and Karen Skidmore – thank you.

Thanks also to Alison Jones and the team at Practical Inspiration Publishing for giving my manuscript the book equivalent of a spa makeover, with copy editing, cover design, formatting, and marketing support. The published book has emerged from this pampering transformed, and Alison's encouragement has been invaluable.

I'd also like to thank my clients, because by trusting me with your books you've allowed me to grow as a writer. I couldn't have written this one without you.

And finally, my gratitude goes to all the other writers who've inspired me to progress in the craft, most of you without knowing it. I always say that good writers tend to have one thing in common: they read a lot. Reading your books has taught me what I know.